PR Power

Inside Secrets from the World of Spin

Amanda Barry

First published in Great Britain in 2002 by
Virgin Books Ltd
Thames Wharf Studios
Rainville Road
London
W6 9HA

ISBN 0 7535 0652 1

Series Consultant: Professor David Storey
Joint Series Editors: Robert Craven, Grier Palmer

Series design by Janice Mather at Ben Cracknell Studios
Typeset by Phoenix Photosetting, Chatham, Kent
Printed and bound in Great Britain by Mackays of Chatham, Chatham, Kent

For my mother, Bettie Alston
And in memory of my father, George PJB Barry

Contents

Acknowledgements

Thanks to Humphrey Price and Kirstie Addis at Virgin for their help and guidance, and to Robert Craven for the opportunity.

To Liz Willmott for assisting with the case studies and reference materials and to Gillian Preston for being my first reader!

Many thanks also to all those who contributed in one way or another, either through interview, advice, feedback or suggestions: Susan Aslan, David Ball, Lisa Betteridge, Michelle Bowey, Caraline Brown, Emma Cantrill, Chris Davies, Tina Durdle, Richard Edelman, Steve Ellis, Annie Garthwaite, Rhodri Harris, Julian Henry, Suzanne Howe, Peter Jones, Tanya Lake, Judd Lander, Liz Lowe, Chris Moss, Ian Muir, Barry Pearson, Stephanie Ponsford, Alan Rushton, Roger St Pierre, Katie Thomas, Julia Wherrell, Will Whitehorn, Professor Paul Whiteley, Peter Willmott and Ian Wright. Thanks also to Emma and Marielle at Metrica Ltd.

Finally, very special thanks to family and friends for their all their support and encouragement over the last year: Ann-Marie Peters, Louise Jackson, Maria Bowers, Kristen Carano, Karen Marsh, Philip Nicholls, Andy, Gillian, Iain, Lisa, Liz and Susan.

Foreword
by Sir Richard Branson

It feels a bit odd to be writing a foreword to a business book. Perhaps it's because I haven't always done business by the book myself. Sometimes I've regretted that, and sometimes I've been glad that I followed my instincts instead of doing what conventional advisers might have recommended.

One thing I've learned is that there's no right way to do things in life. There is no 'magic bullet' for success in business. What works for Virgin Atlantic might not be right for British Airways; what suits your business could be completely wrong for someone else's. But any advice that can help you beat the odds and succeed in business has got to be a good thing. Listening to lots of people's ideas before taking a decision has always been something I have strongly believed in.

Every book in this series has been written by an expert in his or her field, and they've come up with lots of interesting and thought-provoking ideas. But the most important thing is to do what you personally feel is right.

Business should be fun. Enjoy what you do, and success comes within reach.

Good luck!

Preface

If you run a small business you might be tempted to believe that public relations (PR) is something for the big boys. But, whatever the size of your firm, *PR Power* should persuade you that PR is one of the many things that you have to grapple with – good PR can help you; bad PR can destroy you.

Destruction can come in the form of an unexpected call from a journalist investigating a story about your trade or your business, and you being caught on the back foot. Among the many valuable tips in the book is how to handle this type of 'cold call'. Amanda Barry emphasises the importance of giving yourself time to think and, most importantly, collecting information from the journalist and calling them back. Therefore, make sure you always have this book accessible so that, when the call comes, you've got instant access to the 'cold call' tips. It could save your bacon.

But by no means is PR just about crisis management. Instead it is ideally about 'the long game' in which you are able to obtain free positive publicity for your business. It is easily forgotten that journalists have to fill space and that that space will be read by many customers, and potential customers, of your business. So, why shouldn't it be your business that people read about? Helpful journalistic comment is an invaluable marketing tool for the small business and this book helps you to forge a positive relationship with the media.

As far as most small businesses are concerned, the key outlet for positive comment is the regional and trade press. Amanda Barry emphasises just how effective personal links with local and specialised journalists can be for smaller firms. If you respond quickly and helpfully to their requests for information, it is in the journalist's interest to build you up as a reputable firm.

Part and parcel of being media-friendly is the company website. Most journalists will access the site before making contact with the business and first impressions are vital. Here Amanda Barry emphasises the importance of making your site a (positive) statement about the business. Ideally it should be up to date and informative, rather than emphasising high tech wizardry – unless high tech wizardry is your business!

So, don't view PR as something you can do without. At worst, burying your head in the sand can lead to disaster. At best, PR is a great opportunity for you to think through how you want your business to be viewed by others, and to influence the way customers and potential customers view you. And for that you normally pay hefty advertising fees!

Professor David Storey
Director, Centre for Small and Medium Sized Enterprises
Warwick Business School, University of Warwick

Love it or loathe it, Public Relations (PR) is fast becoming one of the most valuable management tools around. If you've ever felt you should be using it – but don't know where to start – or simply wondered what all the fuss is about, then this is the book for you.

I've spent the last fifteen years or so working with many businesses, both large and small, that have sought to unleash the power of PR. Some succeeded, some did not. Those that did had an attitude and approach in common that made them stand apart. I'm now going to share with you the secrets of their and others' success and offer you advice on how you too can start using the incredible power of PR.

Who Is This Book For?

It's for anyone who is interested in understanding more about PR and will be particularly helpful for entrepreneurial businesses with little experience of PR. However, *PR Power* contains advice and ideas that are relevant for all sizes and shapes of business.

How To Use This Book

Designed to be an easy-to-use handbook that can be referred to time and again, you can either choose to complete the toolkit exercises as you go, or read it straight through and go back to the worksheets. Use whatever method suits you best.

What's Next?

If you want to find out more about PR, view some more case studies, or simply share your own PR success stories, click on to the *PR Power* website at www.prpower.info

Step One – PR in a Nutshell |

What is it?

Public Relations is fundamentally the process of managing how, when and in what way you communicate, so that you may ultimately influence the behaviour, attitude and perceptions of those important to you. In our 24/7 business world today, to be able to do this successfully is vital for any business, be it a multinational or one-man band.

But Public Relations – or PR for short – isn't some new fad. The principle of taking charge of how, when and where to communicate with others has been around for as long as humankind has needed to get a message understood. Alexander the Great realised that it wasn't enough just to win battles: you had to let people know about them, too; and so he would send runners ahead to spread news of his victories.

Thanks to technology, we don't have to go to quite the same exhausting lengths to get our messages across, but we must still grapple with the complexities of human interaction in seeking to be heard and understood. Getting the tone, language, approach and timing of how an important piece of news is passed on from one person to the next remains as relevant a process now, as it was in 400 BC.

While our need to communicate effectively may not have changed over the centuries, the way we do business has, of course, changed for ever. Certainly, with the advent of the Internet and the dotcom era, businesses have a window on the world and a direct route to customers that has simply never been possible on such a scale before. We are more accountable, more accessible, more vulnerable than ever before, and managing how we interact with the outside world can no longer be left to chance.

This is where public relations comes in. Effective PR is fast becoming a vital ingredient for many businesses, reflected in the growing investment in this activity on both sides of the Atlantic. In the US alone, the PR industry grew a staggering 32 per cent from $2.3 billion to $3 billion during 2000 (*PR Week,* US edition). So it's important and relevant. But what exactly is it? Unlike other business disciplines such as sales, finance and production, it has a whole range of titles and functions: public affairs, corporate communications, investor relations, publicity departments and press offices, for example, all have special communication remits to fulfil specific needs of an organisation. (Investor relations, for example, manages the communication and relationship between an organisation and its shareholders and their advisers.) Larger businesses often have several of these functions, but all can be fairly brought under the PR umbrella.

For the purposes of this book, though, we will stick to what is perhaps the best-known term, public relations, and its key principles, which are common to all of its specialist areas.

Defining PR

Let's first look at some popular definitions. Public relations is:

- about achieving positive editorial coverage in the media
- the process of engaging the public with your company
- the active management of your communications
- application of strategy and creativity in the management of reputation
- networking with potential clients at seminars, exhibitions and events
- taking important customers and clients to lunch

One of the complexities about PR is that it is all of these things – but never just one of them. As illustrated by the list of different specialist functions we saw above, PR has a very wide field of reference. Taking clients to lunch and getting editorial coverage in your local newspaper are just two activities that contribute to a broader, larger goal, which, as we saw at the start of this chapter, is ultimately about influencing people important to you. The secret of harnessing PR's power is understanding that it doesn't fit neatly into a box, and its influence touches every part of your business, just as the way you communicate does. View the descriptions as jigsaw pieces that go towards making up a completely integrated PR picture and you'll be on your way to grabbing some of that power for your own business.

The Institute of Public Relations in the UK defines PR in this way (which is really a summary of the points listed above): 'Public relations practice is the discipline which looks after reputation with the aim of earning understanding and support and influencing opinion and behaviour.'

Whether it realises it or not, any business is already engaged in PR activity, because it is constantly giving out communication signals. Organisations communicate through brand image, attitude to customers, employee relationships, own-industry activities, local community and so on. By raising the profile of PR within your business, you have simply decided to acknowledge and take charge of, an activity that is already happening all around you.

PR is more complicated than you think and can easily get derailed. Take a few moments now to think about your own experience. Have you undertaken any PR proactively? Was it a good experience? If your experience was less than satisfactory, don't let this put you off getting to grips with it in the future. It's easy to let a negative experience cloud your view. If you've worked with a PR consultancy that didn't deliver what you expected, it may just mean that it wasn't up to scratch. As with dentists, chefs, builders, teachers and so on, the quality of what you get will always depend upon the quality of who's supplying it.

Good PR doesn't merely rely on somebody else to provide the expertise: it also depends upon you. It's true that companies that use PR to the greatest effect are those that take it into the very heart of their organisations. They think, breathe and live PR as an inextricable part of their businesses. Consider those who may be said to have 'great PR' – it's no accident that many are successful entrepreneurs: Charles Dunstone of the Carphone Warehouse, Jeff Bezos of Amazon.com, Richard Branson of Virgin, Stelios Haji-Ioannou of easyJet – all are passionate about their businesses and all understand the immense importance of communication. Not for them a distant

PR department functioning out on a limb: 'PR thinking' is very much part of their everyday business, because they understand that their companies' reputations rely not just on excellent products or services (these are a given) but on the way others – customers, suppliers, employees, shareholders and stakeholders – feel about them, too.

Will Whitehorn, Brand Development and Corporate Affairs Director for the Virgin Group, explains his company's approach to PR: 'We've always put it right in the heart of management decisions because we view it not just as a tool for communicating with the media but as part of how we build and grow the relationship we have with our customers.'

Can you think of a business that you believe has 'good PR'? Do you think it has those general qualities we have looked at above? If so, why? Take a few moments to think about your own organisation:

Amanda Barry's PR Health Check Quiz

- Are there potential PR opportunities that your business could be implementing now?
- Are you confident that your workforce know the goals of the organisation and how their jobs contribute to these?
- Do you know how to measure the effectiveness of PR?
- Do you know what sorts of media (newspapers, magazines, TV, radio, the Net and so forth) your customers and target customers read or view or listen to?
- Could you explain the differences between advertising and PR to someone?
- If you received an unexpected call from a journalist, would you feel confident about handling it effectively?
- If there was a sudden crisis, would your organisation be prepared to deal with it?

If you've answered no to any of these questions, then you and your business need this book! Keep reading and put your PR on the road to recovery.

Why bother?

But why bother to 'manage' communications at all? Don't the facts speak for themselves? Sometimes of course, yes, but more often than not no. Think of personal relationships and how fraught they can be with misunderstandings. We often say one thing and our partners, families or friends may interpret our meaning in a different way from what was intended. If our words and actions can easily be misinterpreted in our private lives, so can they be when the relationship moves to the business arena – with often damaging results. When we *do* leave communications to chance, we need to be prepared for the unexpected – and sometimes a rather undesirable outcome! Communication with the media is a particularly tricky area, as demonstrated in the following example.

Case study: Sober advice

A university based in the North of England undertook a government-funded research programme to study the changing trends in social behaviour. The study was a serious attempt to understand the reasons behind an upsurge in the wine-bar culture and why the traditional Friday night 'lads' night' was now being dominated by women. Press information was duly issued, but those in charge of the programme were aghast at the resulting coverage of it by some newspapers. While the same information had been sent to *The Times* and the *Sun*, the story received a dramatically different treatment. The *Sun* piece, headlined BOOZY BOB'S GOING ON £16,000 PUB CRAWL, not only sent up the whole project by poking fun at the research director, but also slammed the government-backed initiative for wasting taxpayers' money.

While the university had obviously taken pains to communicate the research initiative to the media, its downfall lay in not taking into consideration the different styles and needs of the intended newspaper targets. It is not enough simply to broadcast your version of a story. Everything that is communicated is open to individual interpretation. By thinking through the various audiences with whom you will be communicating, you can anticipate and then minimise the potential for error or misunderstanding.

Ian Wright, group communications director at the drinks giant Diageo, and president of the Institute of Public Relations, believes effective PR is a three-way process. 'There's broadcast and receive and then the third, vital element: what is actually done with the information,' he explains. 'Effective communication will always have some impact on people's behaviour.'

With Boozy Bob in our case study, the university had overlooked this third element, assuming that what they were broadcasting would be received exactly as they intended. Unfortunately, none of us can be certain that this is the case. By using PR thinking from the outset, and actively managing this communication process – as we actively manage finances by working with accountants, or legal issues by gaining expert advice from lawyers – we can maximise our potential for being understood and increase the chances that we will stimulate an appropriate response.

Mind your language
While good PR may not always directly affect the bottom line, it's worth remembering that *bad* PR always does. Remember Gerald Ratner? A few comments made at an industry dinner, when he described one of his company's products as 'crap' – albeit as a joke – effectively destroyed his company's reputation and therefore the company with it. Gerald Ratner may have thought he was communicating with a select few who would understand his comments – but he had forgotten that the media would relay his remarks to a far wider audience, who, in turn, took his words at face value and turned their backs on his stores.

Hitting the jackpot

Sales of 'Big Mouth Billy Bass' the singing fish took off after it was revealed in the national press that the Queen and Tony Blair both had one on their respective mantelpieces.

It was a great PR hit for its manufacturers and distributors, with lots of stories and pictures appearing in the newspapers. Its success was the result of a mixture of good fortune (that such high-profile figures were said to own the novelty) and the fact that it was a great news story (both the head of the royal family and the British prime minister had similar senses of humour).

There's no doubt, though, that this type of PR result leads to greater misunderstanding as to how PR operates. It is precisely because you cannot 'buy' the editorial coverage achieved from this type of exposure that it is so valuable – but by the same token, with no payment for the 'space', it can't be guaranteed to run. It is this element of unpredictability that makes PR such a roller-coaster ride. Had the timing been different or its fans less high-profile, Billy Bass could have sunk without a trace.

Great story + good timing + unpredictability = possible result.

Throughout the book we'll be discussing how, by applying the appropriate planning skills and understanding how the media operate, you can minimise the random nature and maximise the potential for such results.

Living with risk

Learning to live with the possibility of an unknown outcome while doing all you can to influence the eventual result is part of understanding how PR works. Embracing a certain amount of risk is an important part of the process. Many companies take a very defensive approach to PR, particularly when it comes to dealing with the media.

Julian Henry, MD of consumer PR consultancy Henry's House, believes that calculated risk taking is a vital part of getting the best from PR. 'Many companies see PR as a purely defensive tool,' says Henry, 'but working with the media will always have an element of risk to it, so it's better to go with it, than trying to build defensive walls.'

Henry's House works with many clients from the entertainment world, including pop groups such as S Club 7. Henry's House has managed the PR of the group since they were formed and has had to deal with both the good and the bad PR situations that have come their way. During 2000, one tabloid newspaper ran a front-page story about drug taking in the group, with the headline screaming SPLIFF CLUB 7. It was Henry's team that was in the front line when the journalist first called. 'We knew we couldn't stop the story,' says Henry, 'so we got in there and ensured that the facts were correct. We minimised the damage to the group's reputation by working with the journalists to make sure the story was as fair as possible.'

As Henry points out, the drugs story was going to run anyway, so what his team did was to ensure that the communications channels between the pop group and the journalists remained open. The point is that effective PR isn't just about managing the good stories: it's about dealing with the negative ones, too. Ultimately, proactively managed PR will keep those communications links open, even if sometimes the issues are uncomfortable for an organisation to deal with.

Case study: Stimulating debate

When dealing with the media, many companies fall into the trap of viewing PR as simply a means to put out positive stories about their activities and products. This is of course part of the PR function – spreading the 'good news' about a company – but it is only the tip of the iceberg. PR can be highly effective when focusing its activity around issues and stimulating debate that has relevance to its particular cause.

A good example of this is when the trade association for the British aerosol industry, the British Aerosol Manufacturers' Association (BAMA), was faced with a tide of anti-aerosol publicity following the ozone-depletion reports by the British Antarctic Survey in the 1980s: chlorofluorocarbons (CFCs), in widespread use in aerosols at that time, were seen as contributing to the problem. The industry wanted to go to the media with stories on the benefits of the aerosol in a bid to combat the findings of the damming report. However, Grayling PR, one of the PR specialist consultancies approached by the BAMA, advised them to take a different tack.

Chris Davies, MD of Grayling explains, 'It simply wasn't possible to ignore the findings of the British Antarctic Survey and the fact that CFCs in aerosols were definitely not good news for the environment. We proposed, therefore, that the PR campaign should highlight exactly what the industry was doing to remove CFCs, and, most importantly, that it had set its own deadline for compliance with new guidelines for CFC use actually ahead of the internationally agreed one.' By addressing the issue head on, and being seen to be reacting responsibly to it, BAMA effectively 'lowered the temperature' over the issue – and allowed positive messages to be considered.

What about spin?

Spin is to PR what quackery is to the medical profession. Both do damage to the reputation of their bona fide counterparts and often to those who use them. A spin doctor is the rather funky, glib term now widely used by the media to describe anyone involved in communications or PR.

The term was coined in the world of politics, and its meaning is far from complimentary. Spin generally refers to the practice of distorting, adapting or puffing up factual information in order to gain favourable media coverage or convince others of your point of view. Many do use the word innocently, but it does no favours for the serious job of PR. Unfortunately, spinning is a trap that it's easy to fall into, with even its biggest critics, the media themselves, succumbing (each mainstream newspaper has a political leaning and therefore tends to give its own 'spin' to political news reporting).

Of course, there's no reason why politicians or businesses shouldn't put forward their arguments in a positive and persuasive manner; but, when fact strays into fiction, this is where spin begins. Whenever PR is used to cover up unpalatable situations or truths, you know you're in spin country. Hence both the term 'spin' and its practice are at once derogatory and damaging to the whole communications process.

But isn't it right that a company should vigorously draw attention to all the good things about its products or services? What harm is there in embellishing the facts a little? It is right, of course, to promote your business in the most positive and enthusiastic way you can, but it is never OK to step beyond the line of reality. Two parts of the bedrock of effective PR are honesty and trustworthiness – and you ignore these at your peril. Popular perception may be that PR is just the opposite, but, without integrity, we're not talking PR – just a load of old spin.

Dealing with uncomfortable or negative news appropriately is very difficult, and is the reason why some resort to spin, believing it will help get them out of a bad situation. But businesses that do learn to manage the bad issues with honesty and integrity earn the trust and respect of everyone around them, including their customers. It may not be possible to convince everyone of your arguments, but it is possible to strive for a balance between the openness required for good communication and the sensitivity of commercial interests.

Case study: 'Tell Shell'

The Anglo-Dutch oil giant Shell, which was voted 'Britain's Most Admired Company' in the *Management Today* 2001 awards, demonstrated how it is possible to walk this difficult line in its recent dealings with environmentalists and protesters. In the wake of its clash with protesters and its subsequent forced U-turn on the dumping of the Brent Spa oil rig in the North Sea, Shell UK overhauled its entire approach to communications and vigorously took on board the opinions of the public into its operations.

By taking an integrated approach to how it was communicating with those it needed be in contact with – including the fuel-buying public, its employees, shareholders and environmentalists – the company uses its website as an important means of staying in contact with these crucial stakeholders. By providing a dynamic feedback facility within the site – called 'Tell Shell' – it is able to have direct dialogue with protesters and supporters alike, limiting accusations of simply providing 'spin' by wholeheartedly embracing the fuel debate.

What PR can do – and what it can't

One of the thorny issues businesses face when working with PR for the first time is understanding just what it can and cannot do. Remember: those who use PR most effectively are those who not only take its principles to their hearts, but know what a sustained PR effort can do over time.

Five ways PR can help your business

1. Promote understanding between a business and its stakeholders
The benefits of good communication will help develop stronger relationships at every level. The Carphone Warehouse has an enviable employee loyalty reputation, which is well deserved. The company works hard at keeping its workforce motivated and happy with a continual programme of incentives, benefits and strong, internally focused PR activity.

2. Build trust and confidence with opinion formers

These are such people as journalists and potential shareholders – trust is at the very core of most successful relationships. By developing trust and confidence with those who have the power to influence your business, PR creates a channel that keeps communication going through the good and the bad times.

3. Stimulate debate and encourage changes in behaviour, attitudes and perceptions

PR is the persuasion business. By encouraging debate and providing well-thought-out campaigns, PR gives a business the power to encourage a change in others. Professor Paul Whiteley, head of politics at Sheffield University, explains how important the persuasion process is in the world of politics and what factors must be at play for it to be effective.

'Recent research on the psychology of persuasion in politics highlighted three conditions that must be present for effective persuasion to take place,' he says. 'The communicator should firstly be perceived as knowledgeable – voters do not listen to people who they think are ignorant of the issue.

'Secondly, they should be trustworthy. Trust is a key requirement for effective communication to take place. Trust is won over a period of time and becomes a huge asset. If you are trusted, people will be prepared to listen to you and hear you out. In the political world, in the lead-up to the 1997 British general election, Tony Blair was trusted to a much greater extent than he was in the lead-up to the 2001 general election. In his four years as British Prime Minister, he was seen to have let voters down on several issues, so people became disillusioned.

'The third condition for effective persuasion is common-held beliefs. Voters can be persuaded if they think the speaker has similar values and interests as themselves.'

The three criteria for effective political persuasion – knowledge, trust and common interests – have resonance in the business world, too. In the Shell UK case, for instance, where its customers need to feel that the company is aware of the environmental issues, use of these criteria show that the company can be trusted to behave in a way that is sensitive to these concerns and believes in protecting Planet Earth for the future.

4. Mobilise opinion and overcome apathy

PR is used extensively by groups who believe passionately in a cause and want to persuade others to join them. Charities, pressure groups and nongovernmental organisations (NGOs) such as the British Heart Foundation and Amnesty International use PR to gain support and help keep their activities in the public eye.

5. Increase awareness

PR works alongside advertising in pointing out what's special or different about your business/product/service. But, unlike advertising, PR goes a step further by working with third parties – such as journalists – to spread the word on your behalf.

Five things PR can't or shouldn't do

1. Deal in untruths, falsehoods or manipulation

Telling lies won't only make your nose grow longer, it will also put paid to any hope of credibility in the future. Whether you're telling whoppers, as a certain American president did on national TV, or simply saying no when the answer is really yes, remember that effective PR is always built on trust.

2. Operate in a vacuum and ignore valid criticism

The effectiveness of any PR activity is always inextricably linked to the environment in which it is operating, which includes the world inside and outside an organisation. Its power to influence others will also depend upon the climate of opinion and how successful it is in taking on board other points of view, as illustrated by the PR approach we saw taken by Shell UK and the BAMA earlier in this chapter.

3. Be unreliable or inconsistent

Another important factor in good relationships is consistency. As individuals we tend to admire those who behave in a consistent manner. Journalists in particular value a PR contact who is reliable. Andy George, a music journalist, laments the lack of reliability in his own industry.

'It looks bad on a business if they fail to do what they say they are going to do,' he says. 'Often I've been told that a CD for review is in the post, when they have clearly forgotten to send it. So not only is the review opportunity missed because the deadline is passed, it makes them look pretty inept.'

4. Make promises that it can't deliver

There is a current trend among clients towards asking PR specialists to guarantee editorial coverage as part of their contract. While it is certainly good practice to set realistic goals and targeted objectives, it's not possible to *guarantee* coverage unless you pay for it. Then it's called advertising, promotion or advertorial (see Step Three).

5. Encourage unrealistic expectations

This is otherwise known as PR puff. The problem with puff is that, when the reality comes to light, it actually seems more disappointing than maybe it deserves to appear. The challenge with PR is always to look at ways to bring out the benefits of what is already there. When the sportswear specialists Speedo launched their new Fast Skin swim suit to coincide with the Sydney Olympic Games in 2000, the company took care to use four years' worth of research to support their claim that the suit could improve times by up to 3 per cent. An impressive claim that could be supported by hard data.

Puff the PR dragon

PR is used by some as a smokescreen to cover up unsavoury or negative details – or simply to build something out of nothing. To create froth, puff, fancy dressing is a great temptation, but it really must be resisted if you are going to build and sustain any kind of credibility with those you are communicating with – be it customers, journalists, employees, suppliers, even your competitors. Being caught out overstating your case wrecks credibility in an instant. As a customer yourself, how many times have you been disappointed when the new lawnmower, computer, easy-to-assemble desk or instant bread mix turned out to be not quite what you expected when you got it home? The disappointment soon turns to frustration and what should have been a moment of excitement or satisfaction turns into anger at being duped. You may well get away with it once or even twice, but, once confidence is lost, it is very difficult – if not impossible – to win it back.

How can PR be measured?

Because PR deals in many intangibles, it demands its own specific measurement tools. Many become frustrated because it seems impossible to gauge accurately whether their PR efforts have paid off. The problem lies not with measurement but the methods used. It's often a waste of time to measure the results of PR activity directly against short-term sales forecasts, because PR works on changing attitudes and behaviour. It's a slow-burn, long-haul activity that may not necessarily be immediately obvious on the profit-and-loss sheet. There are exceptions, of course, such as when PR is used to achieve awareness for a new product launch and the resulting media coverage stimulates sales. But often the impact of PR demands a more sophisticated method of measurement. We'll be looking at the methods and techniques to use in Step Five.

PR and advertising – understanding the difference

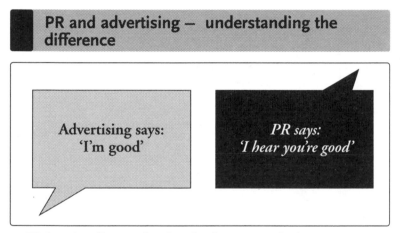

PR is quite often confused with advertising, which is quite surprising, since the fundamental ways in which they work are very different. It's true that both are methods of communication. It's also true that both seek to influence the minds and attitudes of others. But, from thereon in, they take separate paths.

One of the best explanations I've heard of how to describe the differences between PR and advertising is to compare them to a car and a boat. Both are methods of getting you to your destination, but each takes a very different approach. However, when PR and advertising are co-ordinated (as a car and boat may be used at different stages in the same journey), powerful communications campaigns result (see the case study concerning Sega pirate TV below).

PR versus advertising

Advertising is:

- one hundred per cent controlled by the advertiser
- guaranteed to appear in return for payment
- regulated

PR, on the other hand, is:

- directed, but not 100 per cent controlled by the instigator
- not paid for space, so there are no guarantees
- not regulated

In advertising, you pay for the right to display or broadcast your message, be it on a giant billboard, on the side of a double-decker bus, on the page of a magazine or newspaper, on radio or on TV. You can even pay to have your message printed on the food we eat such as eggs, or make your corporate logo an integral part of a product – popular in the fashion world with brands such as French Connection, Nike and Tommy Hilfiger.

In fact, if you've got the spending power, you can pay to get your advert put on just about anything – there are even plans to train giant lasers on the sky so that your advertising message can be projected into space. Advertising is about guaranteeing that your message, which is 100 per cent controlled by you, gets to appear exactly *where* you want it to, *when* you want it to and in the *format* you choose.

PR, on the other hand, is very different and infinitely more frustrating, because it carries no cast-iron guarantees. It is the business of not only getting others to broadcast your message for you, but getting them to do it without expecting any payment in return. PR traditionally must rely on working through a third party, usually journalists, to get its message across to a desired audience. This is a crucial and fundamental difference between advertising and PR and why, when it comes to credibility, PR can blow advertising clean out of the water.

Think of how reviews work. We may see an advertisement for the brand-new Ford car; we may even pause at the page to take a closer look. But it is the 'road-test feature' that grabs our attention. What do the reviewers think? Is it any good? Is the acceleration really going to take my breath away? While we may not always agree with the reviewers' verdicts, we are far more likely to believe what they have to tell us than the manufacturer's own advertisement.

It's not a perfect world, of course, and there are instances when a journalist has a hidden agenda or particular axe to grind. Part of the job of PR is to get round this by getting to know who these journalists are and whether they do have personal bias. If they are doing their job right, they will offer an objective view to help us make up our own minds. It is the job of PR to make sure that the journalist has all the information he or she needs to carry out the review and that these facts are presented in the most informative, relevant and interesting way.

However, like advertising, PR can be only as effective as the quality of the message it is there to impart. Remember that PR is about building trust and providing information with integrity. If your web-design company doesn't have as many big-name clients as your rivals, then focus on other benefits that you offer – such as younger workforce, more competitive rates, area of specialisation or trial-before-you-buy offers. PR is about identifying and making the most of the benefits that are already there, not inventing those you wish you had.

Case study: When advertising and PR are linked

Working in harmony, PR and advertising make a powerful combination. When the computer entertainment giant Sega launched its Mega CD games console to its target audience – cynical, seen-it-all-before teenagers and the world-weary journalists writing for the computer games industry – the company knew it had to do something unexpected to grab everyone's attention.

The advertising campaign kicked off with a series of billboard and magazine ads, promoting two new consumer products: cat food and washing powder. The style of the ads was deliberately corny, with 1950s homemaker-type images and text, and did not make any reference to Sega or the new Mega CD product. The PR campaign was timed so that products' press releases were issued to all the relevant consumer media at the same time, with even a telephone hotline set up for people wanting to know more. Calls were received as people were intrigued by rather bizarre claims on the ads – claims such as that the cat food was 'good enough to eat'.

The press office received several calls from journalists following up the story, with some even requesting interviews with the man pictured in the ads eating the cat food. However, then came the masterstroke of the campaign. Firstly, the posters were 'piratised' overnight – a pirate eye patch appeared over the faces of the corny characters in the advertisements. Then, TV ad spots were taken, which began with the same images and themes of the poster ads – but then they would be suddenly 'taken over' by a fanatical, subversive pirate TV station, with a crazy host talking about the new Sega Mega CD console. The TV ad was one of the longest ever on British TV at that time – designed to reflect the 'epic experience' that gamesters could expect from the console.

At the same time, the billboard ads were also subject to another pirate invasion, with a corner of each ripped off to reveal the pirate TV station's host and information about the Sega Mega CD. When the media realised that they had been caught out and that the whole cat-food/washing-powder campaign was a spoof, there was a flurry of editorial coverage across the national newspapers, the majority of which commented on how clever it had been. Even the more serious business media, who had been curious as to why they had been sent information about the original cat-food/washing-power products, enjoyed the joke and reported it favourably.

The amplification of the ad campaign was just one of the PR tactics used by Sega in the launch of the Mega CD, but it was undoubtedly a brilliant one. By combining the advertising and PR campaigns, the company pulled off a clever coup. By making the advertising campaign the story itself, instead of focusing on the benefits of the product, Sega managed to stimulate a powerful set of responses in its audiences: curiosity, shock, humour and admiration.

Case study: When advertising and PR are not linked

When advertising and PR are not co-ordinated, the opportunity to capitalise on their joint power is lost. Value for money can also be seriously diluted. 3rd Rock Organics was an independent organic-soft-drinks business based in Boston, New England. The company launched a new range of 100 per cent natural fruit juices, targeted at the office-worker snack and lunchtime market. The top of each plastic bottle also served as a mini-cup, which provided the product with its own unique benefit in a quickly overcrowding organic-drink sector. 3rd Rock decided to invest $500,000 advertising the new range and took a major series of ads, featuring real office workers enjoying the drink in the local newspaper, in women's and health magazines and on billboard sites in the city's heavily populated office-block areas.

It was only after the campaign was up and running, however, that the company then briefed its PR consultancy on the project, with just $20,000 left in the budget. Press releases were issued to the drinks trade and target consumer media, and tasting sessions were organised at the local shopping malls and food halls. Some editorial was achieved, although, because many of the magazine deadlines meant journalists were working two months ahead, consumers couldn't read about the drinks until long after they first went on sale.

The trade media did run snippet news pieces, but, largely, the launch went unnoticed. The drink range struggled to gain support from the trade buyers, which meant consumers were not able to buy it and ultimately the range was discontinued.

What could have been done differently here? Had 3rd Rock Organics brought the advertising and PR together from the start, the results might have been far more satisfying. The advertising agency's idea of using real office workers was strong and, by the use of black-and-white photography, the images were striking.

The PR consultancy could have suggested a competition to find candidates for the shoot ahead of the campaign, so that editorial about the ad campaign, the drink range and the chance for ordinary office workers to 'be famous' would have appeared in the local media. The editorial and competition would have created a buzz that would have helped the reps selling the range to the bar, shop and café traders. The unique top/cup feature on the juice bottles could have been offered as an exclusive story to one of the drinks-trade magazines, with information about its development and profile information on 3rd Rock Organics, contributing to the exposure and awareness raising to the trade.

Finally, by co-ordination of the advertising and PR timing schedules, product samples could have been supplied to consumer-magazine journalists in time for editorial to appear just as the advertising campaign hit, thereby providing the greatest impact. The office workers could see the ads, read about the drink and ultimately go into their local snack bar and buy a juice to try for themselves.

Step One summary

- Like it or not, PR is already a force in your business, because every business is constantly communicating with those in and around it. Using PR Power is about taking control of the steering instead of freewheeling along just hoping for the best.

- Public Relations is like a jigsaw – it has lots of pieces that need to be put together to form a complete picture.

- Do what the entrepreneurial giants do and put PR at the heart of your business.

- Effective PR is about taking the rough with the smooth. Learning to deal with bad as well as good news is the sign of a PR-savvy business.

- Bin the spin.

- Don't leave PR out on a limb. Remember that integrating it with advertising and other marketing activities increases value and effectiveness all round.

Step Two – PR Fundamentals |

The PR toolkit

Putting PR into the heart of your business will give you more benefits than you think. By your taking on board its basic principles, PR will not only transform the way your business communicates, but enable you to start taking greater control of the direction you are heading in too.

There are five fundamentals to good PR practice that are the first things to take on board for your journey to PR power. During this chapter we're going to build a toolkit that incorporates these fundamentals and demonstrate how you can apply them to your business.

Before looking at the elements of the toolkit, it's important to establish the framework within which all PR activity should operate. I call this the 'PR values list' and it forms the bedrock of PR effectiveness. Some of the values listed will cause surprise to those who believe that PR is simply there to manipulate and puff up. There's no doubt that some use it in this way and, sadly, there are a few PR experts who are also guilty of less than straightforward practice. Burying the truth behind spin is a dangerous game and likely to backfire.

For businesses interested in using PR to contribute to positive performance, reputation and ability to attract and retain the very best employees, here's my PR values checklist:

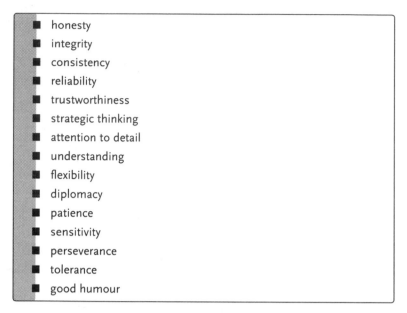

- honesty
- integrity
- consistency
- reliability
- trustworthiness
- strategic thinking
- attention to detail
- understanding
- flexibility
- diplomacy
- patience
- sensitivity
- perseverance
- tolerance
- good humour

How many of the fifteen listed do you recognise from your own experience with PR? If you've run a PR campaign that you feel could have gone better, consider whether it lived up to all of these values. PR can often get derailed because many of the above are not considered as essentials in the PR process.

Preparing your own PR toolkit

The PR toolkit is designed to help businesses develop a framework for proactive PR thinking. Consider each of the five fundamentals in the toolkit and then complete the worksheet activity at the end of each, creating your own customised toolkit.

Toolkit contents

Here are the contents of the toolkit. We'll then look at how each tool is used.

1. **PR antenna** – your own personal radar for picking up and making the most of PR opportunities
2. **Destination and compass** – stated company goals and linked, measurable PR objectives
3. **Area map** – a knowledge of your target customer

4. **Transceiver** – a method of disseminating information to, and receiving feedback from, your workforce
5. **Survival bag** – planning for the unexpected

1. PR antenna – tuning in to PR

Just as some people have a facility for numbers or understanding computers, while others, such as designers, artists and musicians, have a creative flair, so some people have a knack for communication. During the Kosovo crisis in 1999, NATO's spokesman Jamie Shea was widely applauded for his handling of the daily briefings to the world's media. His natural ability as an outstanding communicator enabled him to treat this enormously delicate and difficult task with real skill and sensitivity. Striking just the right balance between authority and compassion, officialdom and man-on-the-street, Shea's handling of the situation meant he would happily put a tick against every single one of the PR values list above.

Of course, it's not possible for everyone to be a great communicator, but it *is* possible to become a better one. By developing greater awareness of what's going on outside the immediate demands of the day-to-day pressures, businesses can lock on to PR opportunities that come their way. One of the key benefits of working with a PR consultancy is that the best ones have plenty of natural communicators, who combine these innate talents with specialist knowledge and skills such as crisis management and media-relations practice.

Even if you do have access to external expertise, however, developing your own early-warning system is a great way to keep PR focused.

Jamie Shea had a unique communications challenge because of the nature of the information he was imparting and he certainly didn't have a problem getting attention for what he had to say. Most businesses however have to work a bit harder to grab the headlines. By using information and opportunities that already exist, you can improve the chances of attracting media attention to your own particular story. Tuning into what's going on either locally, nationally or worldwide and then seeing if there's an opportunity to hop on the back of it with your own news is what developing your own PR Antenna is all about.

Case Study: One step ahead

A good example of this is Amnesty International's use of the Chinese President's October 1999 visit to the UK to communicate its messages. The world's largest human rights organisation, Amnesty International seized the opportunity of this major state visit to highlight China's human rights situation.

As media attention would be on President Jiang Zemin's visit for the whole week, Amnesty International issued a press release and detailed media briefing about China and human rights the week prior to the visit. This established human rights as an important issue with journalists even before Jiang's arrival and lead to pre-visit features in the *Daily Express, Guardian* and *Independent.*

In the week of the visit, as the various TV crews waited for a glimpse of the President, Richard Bunting, Amnesty International's Head of Press offered to be interviewed by the crews to comment on the situation. This led to a piece on the news on Channel 5. Later that night, BBC2's *Newsnight* ran a 'Day in the Life' piece, shadowing Richard Bunting in his efforts to generate media coverage and contrasting this with Jiang Zemin's itinerary. This was followed by a live in-studio debate about Human Rights and China.

As the week progressed, the Metropolitan Police tried to shield Jiang Zemin from peaceful protestors, serving as a further opportunity for Amnesty International to get across its messages. Richard Bunting explains: 'The police's methods highlighted the lengths the British Government was prepared to go in shielding the Chinese President from criticism. We believe this tactic backfired, actually leading to more press coverage, which only served to keep the debate going, offering Amnesty International further opportunities to comment.'

Throughout the visit, Amnesty International worked hard to stay one step ahead of the Government in winning the battle to get their point of view covered by the media. According to Richard Bunting, 'We used good forward planning with rapid reaction to take advantage of events as they unfolded. We believe that this, combined with errors made by the government and Metropolitan Police in handling the situation, led to sustained media coverage, which emphasised our human rights concerns.'

In all, Amnesty International was featured in thirty pieces of national press coverage, twenty national television pieces and seventeen national radio items, and achieved its main aim of keeping human rights as a central part, publicly and politically, of the state visit for the entire week.

Amnesty International's approach illustrates how it's possible to achieve results by hopping on to something that is already happening – though the subject doesn't have to be quite so high profile or controversial for your business to take advantage of an opportunity.

Toolkit Exercise 1 – Switching on your PR antenna

Go and buy a selection of today's newspapers. Give yourself twenty minutes to flick through them all. As you do, think about how your business/products/services may relate to other wider topics that are being reported in the papers. Look at the news stories and features – what topics are popular? Can you adapt what your business has to say to what's already causing a stir?

Tear out anything that grabs your eye and start to compile a cuttings reference file for your desk. Do repeat the exercise on a regular basis, and include the Sunday papers now and again.

The same principle applies to your own and, of course, your customers' trade press. What topics are hot right now? Does your business have something to contribute to an ongoing debate?

Look also at regional newspapers and business publications – is there something happening locally that you can tap into? Helping the local community also brings many benefits to all concerned – for instance, a local car hire firm might provide free minibus hire to a kids' playgroup after reading about the theft of the playgroup vehicle just before a planned visit to the seaside. Good story, good photo, branding opportunity for business, great day out for the kids. Being opportunistic isn't a sin if it provides a win-win situation all round – enhancing your company's reputation, while giving genuine value to your customer.

And baby came too ...

During the height of the GM food debate, the baby-food manufacturer Baby Organix made the most of the moment by taking 'behind-the-scenes' photographs from its new advertisement. Cute pictures of baby covered in food may not be new, but, owing to the intense media interest in anything organic, the picture story earned Baby Organix a big splash in a leading British tabloid newspaper and lots of valuable publicity for its range of baby foods.

---

2. Destination and compass – know where you're going and stay on course

Management books are full of advice on setting goals – and for good reason. Anyone who has bothered to do so knows how powerful the exercise is. Not only because it makes perfect sense to give some thought to where you are heading, but also because you want to know how far you have come and what progress has been made. Business mentor and consultant Robert Craven's mantra of 'If you don't know where you're going then any road will do!' brings home the point. In PR, it is all too easy to get caught up with the actual doing – sending out press releases, dreaming up clever stunts to grab attention, holding grand launch events – that the questions 'What are we doing this for?' and 'What is our main objective?' can be lost or not even considered at all beyond the immediate short-term result.

I have been asked to undertake campaigns for clients who have not thought past the idea that they 'want to do some PR'. Bizarrely, they are prepared to invest time and money in this activity without making the link between this activity, their overall company goals and specific PR/communication-oriented objectives.

One client was very keen to undertake PR, but, while they were enthusiastic at the start, PR was always seen as simply an 'add-on' activity. It was only during a media training session (when we were putting executives into simulated media interview situations) that it became clear that only the chief executive of the company knew what the business goals actually were. The rest of the senior management certainly didn't and we were left tinkering around the edges. The PR activity stalled because not only were these goals and objectives not being shared, but the PR was expected to operate in a vacuum, achieving superficial results, but not addressing the core of the issues at hand.

So first establish what your business goals are. The PR goals will filter down from these. Once you've set the PR goals, then decide how you will measure your progress. For example, Picture This, a framing business with two profitable retail outlets (turnover £1.2 million), was facing increased competition from a new out-of-town shopping complex. Not only would the complex draw customers away from the town centre, but also a rival framing business had taken a unit there.

Picture This had three key business objectives:

1. retain existing customers and combat threat of new competition
2. increase customer base by 10 per cent
3. grow profits to 20 per cent of turnover

The linked PR objectives were

1. achieve editorial coverage for Picture This in local newspapers and magazines to raise profile of products and special offers to local shoppers
2. stimulate debate in local media to promote high street shopping and underline importance of survival of town centre stores to community
3. devise creative campaign to encourage more people to get their pictures and photographs framed professionally

PR measurement criteria:

- target number of editorial pieces
- customer questionnaire, before and after campaign, to gauge attitudes to high street shopping (this may also provide data to support high street shopping argument)
- data-capture system at point of sale for recording where customers had heard about Picture This

Picture This had established clear objectives for both the business and its PR campaign, together with a method for evaluating the success of the activity. By creating clear guidelines from the outset, you can keep your PR focused upon the real issues facing the business.

Toolkit Exercise 2 – Establish goals and method of measurement

(i) If you have already gone through the process of establishing what your business goals are, write them out below. If not, then take some time now to think through what these are. It's important for the purposes of this PR Toolkit exercise, to keep them simple and succinct, as in the example we saw above.

My business goals for the next twelve months are:

_____

_____

_____

_____

(ii) Consider the potential impact that PR activity could have on each goal, scoring the level of this impact between 0 and 3.

	Potential Impact of PR
Goal 1 _____	0 = none
Goal 2 _____	1 = some
	2 = significant
Goal 3 _____	3 = major

(iii) Now, bearing in mind your own scoring system above, set out below, three or four relevant PR/Communication goals for your business, that link to these overall business goals (for example, think about issues such as raising awareness, communicating to particular audience/stakeholder groups, influencing favourable attitudes or behaviour in relation to the business). Be as specific as you can e.g: increase customer response by 5 per cent, raise awareness of issue by 20 per cent etc. Remember, however, that, in order to know if you have been successful, you'll need to know what your starting point is – we'll be discussing in Step Five how to do this.

PR/communication goals (I have indicated three goals as this is a good number to focus on. There is no hard-and-fast rule, but do keep it realistic.)

Goal 1 _____

Goal 2 _____

Goal 3 _____

(iv) Measuring progress and results:

Later in the book (Step Five), we'll be looking in more detail how PR can be measured and the various methods available for doing so. Therefore, this part of the Toolkit will be easier to complete once you have this information at your fingertips. For the time being, if you have undertaken PR activity, simply record here what method (if any) was used to monitor and evaluate it:

Was this method satisfactory? If not, why?

---

3. The area map – know the terrain you are dealing with

It sounds an obvious point that you should know who your customers are, but in practice it's easy to be quite vague about who it is you are actually targeting. To make your PR efforts count, it's vital to know who it is you are trying to reach. PR, like advertising, works at its best when it is sure of its target. This could be as broad as 'all 25–50-year-olds', such as are targeted by the British Heart Foundation in its fight against coronary heart disease. Or all of Severn Trent Water's 8 million Midlands-based customers targeted with a specific campaign to raise awareness of the company's involvement in environmental activities.

Then you need to consider which communication channels to use, be it through the national press, trade publications, regional newspapers and radio, the Internet or environments such as specialist-interest clubs and groups, bars and clubs, restaurants, retail outlets. If your target customer is another business, it's important to consider routes to reaching individuals within that organisation through what media or activities they may be personally exposed to. Part of the creative process of PR can be to find innovative ways to target an audience. In the run-up to the 1997 general election in the UK, New Labour put up signs in pub and club toilets with the slogan NOW WASH YOUR HANDS OF THE TORIES. It was a clever route to getting their message across to younger audiences in an unexpected environment.

Case Study: Hitting the target

An innovative approach in reaching its customers was used by the drinks giant Matthew Clark. It needed to boost declining bottle sales of its brand-leading premium cider Diamond White and to increase the all-important street cred of the brand among its 18–24-year-old C1/C2/D male and female target audience. The company's PR agency, GCI/Jane Howard, part of GCI London group, devised *The Diamond White Buzz Zone* – a weekly review of the core areas of interest to this group (music, sport, film celebrity and fashion), which had been brought to light by pre-campaign research. Using top journalists to compile the information and then persuading five key local radio stations around the country to carry the unique bespoke programming slots, it created a powerful method of communicating credibility for the Diamond White brand. This in turn, contributed to a reverse in the sales decline by the achievement of 13 per cent year-on-year growth.

Toolkit Exercise 3 – Know your target audience

Being clear about whom your PR activity needs to target will help keep the PR effort focused and appropriate. Take a few minutes now to log the target audiences for your business, including trade groups as well as consumers. There may be several groups, each requiring a specific PR approach. It may not be possible due to budget or resource issues, or even appropriate, to target all so use this exercise to score these groups in order of priority bearing in mind your overall business goals and current available resources.

Target audience/stakeholder groups

Group 1 _____

Group 2 _____

Group 3 _____

Group 4 _____

Target Audiences
0 = little relevance
1 = some relevance
2 = significant relevance
3 = major relevance

The next step is to gather as much information about the audience(s) as possible so that your PR activity is focused. In the case-study example above, Diamond White included a research element into its PR campaign, gaining valuable information about its 18–24-year-old audience, which shaped the nature of the PR activity. Professional organisations and associations often have industry data available for their members, or your own business may already have conducted research at product-development stage. Gather together as much as you can – the more you know about your audiences, the better you will be able to tailor your communication with them.

For example, could you answer the following in relation to your target groups?

- What media (magazines, trade journals, newspapers, TV programmes and so forth) are they exposed to/interested in?
- What are their interests?
- What age group/sex/geographical area are they from?

4. Transceiver – sharing information with and receiving feedback from your workforce

If employees feel valued by an organisation, and if their needs are attended to and they have the information they need to accomplish their jobs, their productivity and motivation to work will be high. Positive internal communications have an important role to play in achieving good employee relations. By putting the spotlight on to the why, when and how this communication should take place, PR can help unlock the great benefits of an informed and involved workforce.

Employees are walking, talking ambassadors of any organisation. Companies that are held in high esteem by their employees enjoy an incredible advantage over their competitors precisely because these opinions really can't be bought. Of course, good salaries will always attract good people, but it's the working environment and culture that often flex the most muscle when it comes to making your people stay when a bigger offer comes along. And it's worth remembering that the word-of-mouth passing on of personal experiences resonates more clearly than any glossy ad, clutch of awards or company brochure.

Corporate Advisory Services (CAS), specialises in providing

strategy and communications advice to many FTSE and Fortune 100 companies, with experience in reputation management. Research by CAS into what influences corporate reputation produced a sobering result. The most powerful influencer was television, but a close second came the attitude and behaviour of employees, who carry the most power to affect, either positively or negatively, how a company or brand is viewed by its audiences and stakeholders.

Case study: Carphone Warehouse

The Carphone Warehouse (CPW) chooses to use an in-house magazine as one way of communicating with its 4000 plus employees. The company, winner of several industry awards for employee relations, including *Retail Week*'s 'Employer of the Year' in 1999 and 2001, understands the need to maintain strong communications, especially while the business was experiencing a period of major change in the run up to its becoming a public limited company.

CPW has invested time and budget in keeping the magazine relevant and fresh, which has proved to be a key factor in its continuing popularity with the workforce. Called *In The Know* (*ITK*), it was relaunched by the CPW's PR consultancy, GCI London in 1999, following feedback from employees asking that the magazine involve them, while still having the look and appeal of a mainstream consumer publication.

The objective for *ITK* was simple. It needed to provide employees with a source of company news while reinforcing positive company values and messages. The challenge therefore was to create a publication that reflected the young, team-orientated dynamism of the CPW culture, while communicating key business and motivational messages. It also required a real call to action for the 19–30-year-old workforce who were passionate about customer service and knew their products – but also loved to party.

This was achieved by involving the CPW employees at every opportunity. Each issue features an employee on the cover; the contents are a balance between information from the business – news and features on departments and developments – and more light-hearted regular columns. These include Out & About, a showcase of some of the best company social events – from the Swindon store Friday night out to the annual Company Ball.

Employees are invited to write/email in and request a camera so that they can become an *ITK* spy for the night. There is also The Dating Game. CPW is a social company with a lot of young, free and single types, so a matchmaking series run on the company intranet has employees voting who should go on a date with whom. The final result gets showcased in *ITK*. CPW believes in inspiring its employees to go all the way to the top and strive for excellence, so, in Job Centre, *ITK* spotlights the people who have – showing their contribution to the business and their own personal route to success. There is also Regional Focus: with stores across the UK and into Europe it's important that ITK carries regional company stories that will appeal to everyone. And Cover Mounts & Giveaways: for that added consumer feel, ranging from lollipops and herbal teas to tickets to The *Cosmo* Show. Each freebie is carefully selected to appeal to the target market.

An annual communications audit means that *ITK* is constantly being assessed to ensure that objectives are being met and that employees are happy with their company magazine. Recent research carried out among over 4000 CPW employees as part of the most recent audit revealed that readers give the new look *ITK* an average of 8 out of 10, compared with the 4.5 that was awarded to the magazine prior to the revamp.

Toolkit Exercise 4 – Keeping in touch with your workforce

By extending your PR thinking to include how you are communicating with your team, you will be able to tap into this very powerful resource. If PR is about influencing attitudes and behaviour in others, then directing its beam internally as well as externally isn't just good for morale: it impacts on performance potential, too. Internal communication must be moved from the 'soft' would-be-nice-if-we-find-time-to-do-it issue to an essential element in business strategy and planning.

Look at the checklist below of the most common ways businesses keep the information flow going internally. The larger the organisation, of course, the more complex the internal communication challenge is – but, whether a business employs five or five thousand people, the essential principles remain the same: *listen, involve* and *respond.* Remember that you already have at your disposal one of the most-powerful, and often the most-overlooked, management tools of all – that of leading by example. So if you want an organisation that communicates well and effectively, it's up to you to set the standard! Consider which of the following would be the most appropriate for your organisation by scoring the potential effectiveness of each:

Internal PR Tools

☐ one-to-one and group briefings
☐ employee newsletters, newspapers or magazines
☐ employee-dedicated TV-channel broadcasts
☐ internal reports and information booklets
☐ focus groups (provide 'safe' environment for employee feedback)
☐ Internet sites (including web and intranet sites)
☐ videos and audio tapes
☐ email messages and online newsletters
☐ suggestion schemes
☐ communal area notice boards

Internal PR Tools

0 = no use
1 = some use
2 = significant use
3 = major use

You may already be using internal communication tools, but only in 'broadcast' mode. Using your scoring system above as reference, write out below two or three possible ways to open up the dialogue with your workforce and how an element of feedback could be included:

_____

_____

_____

_____

There's a Chinese saying:

Tell me and I forget
Show me and I remember
Involve me and I understand

Businesses that involve will evolve – and take their workforce with them.

Look who's talking

Even in very small businesses, making sure there is regular two-way communication between the management and staff is vital. For example, round-the-table team updates, having individuals give a snapshot view of what their priorities are that particular week and highlight any issues that may affect the whole team is how we structured it at my consultancy, ABC. The updates were also used to keep the team informed of progress on company issues such as new business, marketing, training and recruitment. We also had a 'newspaper cutting of the day' system, whereby everyone chose at least one important, interesting or quirky story or photo from that day's newspapers and put it up on the company notice board. This helped us keep abreast of the mammoth task of sifting through each day's media mountain and report back interesting opportunities to our clients. It was also an important element in each individual's contribution to the team effort.

---

5. Survival bag – planning for a rainy day

How a company acts in the face of a single disaster or major problem often carries more weight than years of exemplary behaviour. No matter what size a business is, negative or crisis issues can arise out of nowhere and pose a real threat to reputation and survival. More and more organisations appreciate the very real danger in responding inappropriately or slowly to a crisis. Even businesses that don't have factories, warehouses or large-scale workforces to worry about are of course just as likely to suffer when things go wrong, be it with the products or services they are supplying, dissatisfied customers or hostile media attention.

Case study: Total recall

When the US healthcare giant Johnson & Johnson decided to recall more than 31 million bottles of its product Tylenol, at a cost of $100 million (£71.4 million) following the deaths of seven customers, the FBI thought the move unnecessary. The product was found to contain cyanide and, although investigations proved that the substance was added after manufacture, Johnson & Johnson knew that its most valuable commodity – the trust held in it by its customers – was at stake and went ahead with the recall anyway, alerting customers to the danger. The result was that public confidence remained intact and the company's other brands were unaffected by the scare.

Even Tylenol itself, previously holding the market top spot with 35 per cent, which slumped in the immediate aftermath of the scare, bounced back to 30 per cent market share just one year later. The incident happened in 1982 and is now described as one of the greatest business decisions of all time – setting a precedent in crisis management. It was a brilliant example of how, in the face of a devastating crisis, a company that reacts quickly, honestly and effectively can emerge with its reputation unscathed.

While it isn't appropriate for a smaller business to spend large amounts of time and money working through crisis scenarios – as corporations in high-risk sectors such as the healthcare, oil and transport industries must do – it is important to take time to think the unthinkable. How would your business respond when something seriously goes wrong?

A basic rule of thumb in any PR-related activity is always to think before you act, and this is never more appropriate than when you are faced with a hostile or difficult situation. Of course, it's not possible to predict exactly what problem may arise, but, by taking the worst-case scenario and considering how it would be handled, a business dramatically increases its chances of riding out the storm.

MD's juggling act

Anyone who runs a business knows it can be like trying to spin a set of plates on sticks all at once: you get one going perfectly and the next one goes all wobbly. Straighten that one and there goes another, and so on. The odds are that, sooner or later, one of those plates is going to slip and crash. PR thinking can't stop the plates from falling, but it can help you anticipate that possibility and plan how to recover your poise more quickly if they do.

Toolkit Exercise 5 –What's the worst that can happen?

Crisis management – the four basic rules

Rule 1: Consider all possibilities

What could go wrong? Defective products, fire or flooding in your promises, employee injury or death? As with insurance policies or legal contracts, it's best to assume the worst even though the odds are against its happening. After all, 'unsinkable' was the major part of the *Titanic*'s marketing blurb.

Take a few minutes now to jot down three or four crisis scenarios that could happen to your business. Remember: a real crisis will make you break out in a cold sweat just thinking about it!

i) _____

ii) _____

iii) _____

iv) _____

Now consider whether your organisation is equipped to manage the fallout from these examples. Communication systems are one of the most important to protect during a crisis, since communicating is precisely what you must continue to do should there be a major problem.

Ready or not?

- How easy would it be for you to contact key personnel outside work hours should a crisis emerge?
- Can they contact you?
- Do you have a spare telephone line that can be used if all the existing lines are clogged up with customers/journalists/shareholders wanting to know what's going on?
- How quickly would you be able to prepare a statement that could be issued to the media/public to let them know that you are dealing with the situation?
- Do you have a reliable backup facility for your computer system should the data files be lost or stolen?
- Is there an off-site facility for valuable documentation?

Rule 2: Be prepared for what to say

Prepare some Q&As – questions and answers – that will enable you to consider what your response might be to difficult questions. Consider an issue your business is currently facing – say the installation of a new warehouse, distribution or computer system, a move to new premises or internal reorganisation. Now think of five or six questions that stakeholders – those with an interest in your business and its future – may like to ask. If you are already working with a PR consultancy, get them to help you work through the list. Remember to include some questions that you never want to face, and then come up with an answer.

i) _____

ii) _____

iii) _____

iv) _____

v) _____

This is a useful exercise to do prior to even the most innocuous event such as attendance at an exhibition or factory opening; but, whatever you do, don't sit there with your Q&As in front of you. I had one client who, in the middle of an interview with a particularly difficult trade journalist, pulled out his Q&A notes and began reading from them! I managed to swipe them away before the journalist could lean over and see what else was on the list, but the client did look rather silly. So Q&As are homework only. You don't need to be word-perfect, just confident that you are prepared.

Rule 3: Learn from the experts

Do media training. Facing a barrage of questions from journalists can be tough at the best of times, so do yourself a favour and get some training in now. In the meantime, take a look under the heading 'The media interview' in Step Three and also 'Handling cold calls' in Step Six for some advice on talking to journalists.

Rule 4: Remember to communicate

Keep stakeholders in the picture: remember to keep communicating with all those with a vested interest in the outcome of a particular problem. 'No comment' or a wall of silence actually speaks volumes (saying, for instance, 'We don't know what we're doing', or 'We're running away from the issue'), so try to avoid going into the bunker. But do be careful how you do choose to communicate difficult news.

One blue-chip CEO decided to use the company voice-mail system to inform staff of coming redundancies. It may have seemed more efficient – after all, there is no easy way to give bad news – but the insensitivity of the approach will linger around long after employees have cleared their desks.

Outside-hours list

The nature of crises is that they usually happen on a bank-holiday weekend or even in the middle of the night. Identify key personnel who would need to be informed immediately anything happens. The list shouldn't be a long one, and should be circulated only to those who are on it, since it will probably contain home telephone numbers. Remember to revise it when people are away on holiday. Establish who is the spokesperson and ensure that it is only that person who speaks to the media should the need arise.

Step Two summary

- Remember the PR Values List and use it to help your business communicate positively and productively.
- Treat the five fundamentals as your PR bare necessities and remember that whilst we can't all be great communicators, we can always be better ones.

Step Three – PR in Action |

When most people talk of 'getting some PR', what they usually mean is that they want some positive editorial exposure in the media. Known as press or media relations, this is undoubtedly the high-profile part of the job and often the most challenging. Whether a business hires a PR consultancy to manage this task for it or runs the function in-house, it's important to understand some basic principles of how media relations works and why it sometimes doesn't deliver quite what you expect.

This chapter explores the PR–journalist relationship and takes a look at the tools and persuasion techniques used by PR experts to achieve the Holy Grail of non-paid-for, positive editorial coverage.

The 24/7 media world

We live in a world where there is wall-to-wall communication and, as a business, you have no choice but to be part of it. This is one of the key reasons why PR – the art of managing your communications – has become so vital to a successful, growing business. With the addition of the Internet – with nearly a billion users worldwide, and counting – we do rather have the world at our fingertips, and it's a world that is eager to communicate with us. Ian Muir, MD of Strategy PR, believes the relevance of the media for business has never been so vital. 'There's no escaping the impact that the media may have on a business, be it either from a negative or positive perspective,' he explains. 'There is a three-hundred-and-sixty-degree vision of everything we do that simply wasn't the case ten or even five years ago.'

Regional media have become particularly important to the small and medium-sized businesses with the impressive audience share and continued popularity of regional newspapers, and with the advent of cable and satellite television.

Reasons to go regional
Eighty-four per cent of all British adults (40 million people) read a regional newspaper, compared with 68 per cent who read a national newspaper. Since 1999, regional press coverage has grown by 1.4 per cent and total readership has increased by 907,000, while national press coverage has fallen by 3 per cent (down by 1,651,000 readers). Regional newspapers have a high proportion of readers (41 per cent) who don't read a national newspaper. (Source: BMRB/TGI 2001 & www.newspaper-soc.org.uk)

It's now possible to experience directly the impact TV coverage can have on a company because of the accessibility of local-news TV channels whose remit is to cover stories from businesses in their own geographical area. With over 300 satellite, cable and digital TV stations broadcasting across the UK, we're now becoming spoiled for choice. In addition, as national TV in the UK fragments, along the lines of channels across Europe and in America, the opportunity for reaching tailored audiences is unprecedented. The Carlton Food Network and the European Business Channel are just two examples of TV stations now dedicated to niche interests. They welcome ideas and input from businesses who have products or services that are of relevant interest to their viewers.

The PR–journalist relationship

Media relations is rather like the cultivation of a tree. It takes time, resources and patience for the results to begin to show, but, if you tend it well, it will grow, establish firm roots and continue to blossom year after year. As with most things, you must first do the groundwork before you can see the results. Media-relations work is an excellent illustration of the law of reaping what you sow in practice.

A colleague who works for a major blue-chip company relates a story about how his hard work at being consistently trustworthy and constantly accessible to journalists paid off. 'We make it a policy to be available to take calls from the media on a twenty-four-hours-a-day, seven-days-a-week basis,' he says, 'and I regularly take calls up to nine or ten p.m. on a Saturday, when they're preparing the pages for the Sunday papers. This support's paid off, because, when a damaging and incorrect rumour about my organisation emerged late on one Saturday afternoon, I was able to call all of the city editors on the Sunday newspapers and warn them not to take it seriously. Because we hadn't misled them before and had built up a bank of trust and reliability through our previous actions, they were able to be confident that the information I was giving them was correct. Not one ran the story.'

It may not be appropriate for you to offer such unlimited access to journalists, but the principle of being readily accessible remains the same. One of the key principles I always encouraged my clients to adhere to is that calls from journalists need to be treated as a priority. It's no good expecting a journalist to write a story about your company if you're not prepared to adapt your own priorities to meet theirs.

WWW – the Three Golden Ws of media relations

The basic premise of the media-relations task is simple. In order to get what is required (favourable editorial coverage), it is the job of the communicator (you or your appointed PR expert) first to make sure you meet the needs of the journalist. This may seem the wrong way around. Shouldn't the journalist be interested in what you have to say, anyway? Well, yes and no. The classic complaint by many journalists is that they are constantly bombarded with information that is either irrelevant or inappropriate for their readership/audiences. A national newspaper journalist can receive up to 200 press releases a day, so, if you get irritated by the few bits of unsolicited mail that drop through your letterbox, imagine receiving this amount – and knowing that you've probably got to take a look at each one, just in case it does happen to be of interest. It's a basic point, but one that a staggering number of companies and so-called PR experts don't bother to get right.

Neglecting to target your message accurately in the first place is like giving a seminar about the joys of potholing, only to find you are addressing the claustrophobics' convention by mistake. It just wastes everybody's time and probably upsets a few along the way too. While it isn't vital or necessary to get to know personally every journalist who may be interested in what you have to say, it is vital to understand what their needs are so that you are able to communicate with them effectively.

Another common mistake is for an MD or CEO to expect the media to revolve around their own personal timetable. This is not only arrogant, it misses the point that PR is about building relationships that are trustworthy, consistent and respectful. Unless you are a genuinely big cheese such as the Queen or Madonna, most of us need to fit into the schedules set by the media. By working to accommodate the needs of the journalists you are trying to reach, they will in turn appreciate your efforts and a stronger relationship is built between you.

By adopting the following core principles (which I call the Three Golden Ws) when undertaking media relations you will ensure that your chances of achieving editorial coverage and establishing good relations with the journalists are off to a good start.

- **Why** is what we have to say of interest? Is it news? Is it relevant to their readership or audience?

- **When** is their deadline for accepting information? Is it a daily, weekly or monthly publication? If it arrives with the journalist too late, you'll miss their deadline and your information will be put off to the next issue or dropped completely. However, needless to say, it will be very unhelpful to your cause if you bug a journalist just as they are right on deadline, so bear this in mind when you make your approach.

- **What** format do they require the information? Journalists usually have a preference for how they like to receive material: for example, by post, fax or email. If you get this wrong, at best your information will annoy, at worst it won't reach them at all. Sometimes a more personal approach is appreciated. Sending a press release out to everyone at once is all very well, but, if your database isn't bang up to date, then many will miss their targets.

Taking the time and effort first to contact journalists individually by phone and then to forward the release if they are interested enables a more tailored approach. Calls should be brief and to the point – no waffling allowed.

Worksheet: The Three Golden Ws

Take a few moments now to think about something you feel is news-worthy about your business or its services/products and apply the Three Golden Ws principle to it.

1. What is it? For example: new product launch, service innovation, new member of staff, business expansion.

_____

_____

_____

2. What type of media do you think would be interested in the story? Trade publication, specialist magazine, local newspaper, national media? It could be more than one of these.

_____

_____

_____

3. Why will they be interested? Try to think as objectively as possible about this point. It is a crucial part of getting your approach on target.

_____

_____

_____

4. What deadlines do they work to? If it's a monthly publication, you may have just missed their cut-off point for accepting new material. It's a PR adviser's job to know this, but it's a good idea to have some

idea yourself on how the most important media to your business operate. For example, if you are a restaurant, does the local newspaper have a regular entertainment-and-leisure supplement or listings? If you are an Internet business, titles such as *New Media Age* may be important to you, so it makes sense to find out when and how they accept PR information.

_____

_____

_____

5. How do they prefer to accept PR information? Fax, post or email? It usually takes a little desk research to find this out – and something that a PR consultancy or in-house expert will already know or carry out on your behalf. For example, when approaching TV or radio programmes, sending a short, punchy fax or email that gives a brief summary of what you want to say is more likely to get a response than a standard blanket press release.

_____

_____

_____

Hold the front page!

Occasionally you see a national newspaper change its front page overnight because a really big story is breaking just before the paper hits the presses. When the British Tory MP Michael Portillo revealed his gay experiences as a youth during a run-of-the-mill newspaper interview in 1999 (this was before he was re-elected to the Commons in a by-election, having lost his seat in 1997), all hell broke out in Fleet Street as newspaper editors scrambled to rewrite their entire front-page stories for the following day's papers. First editions were already on hold, awaiting the result of a crucial England-versus-Poland football match, due to end after the traditional front-page news deadline. Big news though a key international England football match is to the British press, the Portillo story kicked it easily into touch.

Great expectations

The game of media relations is a tough one and unreal expectations can be a major obstacle to making it work for you. Here are some rules of thumb to bear in mind.

■ Not all of your stories will get used, even if you do adhere to the Three Golden Ws rules. Stories get bumped off the page when something bigger or better comes along – which can range from celebrity scandals to war reporting. Newspaper editors are in the business of selling newspapers and will tailor their coverage accordingly.

■ Your competition will get mentions that you think you should have had, sometimes because they are more adept at PR than you and because you didn't get back to the journalist in time for their deadline (see the Three Golden Ws above). Sometimes it's just because their story is better than yours.

■ You can't be everywhere, all of the time and to get upset about it is just wasted energy and reveals an unreal expectation of how the world works.

■ Simply saying something doesn't make it so – it can take time for your message to be heard. Even Margaret Thatcher had to bide her time before she got listened to.

■ You won't get into every article that is relevant to your business.

■ Successful PR also means sometimes keeping stories out of, as well as in, the media.

■ You won't win the hearts and minds of your customers instantly – or journalists, for that matter. It can take months, even years, of consistent pounding to be registered at 'top of mind' by journalists in your area of industry.

■ If you have big expectations of PR, you need to fulfil them with an attitude and budget to match. It takes the risk of being first, a budget that matches or exceeds your competitors, time for it to work and understanding of how it operates so you don't abandon the effort of a successful campaign just because you don't hit all of your targets straightaway.

Persistence pays off

When working for Motorola's European Paging Division in the mid 1990s, ABC was targeted with achieving major editorial coverage in the *Financial Times* for Motorola's new paging protocol, FLEX. It took nearly eighteen months of putting forward stories and ideas, working with the journalists to research information for smaller news stories, making sure Motorola spokespeople were accessible to provide industry comment when approached by the journalists (usually within hours of their deadline), until we were finally able to achieve this goal. Motorola were also able to provide all of the ingredients necessary to get a major feature like this. They were first (by launching an industry-wide report into trends and attitudes towards paging protocols), vulnerable (they had to talk about the problems faced by Motorola in gaining acceptance of their new standard) and they had news (another European country had signed up to the protocol). But, most of all, faith in the PR process meant that the company's executives made it a priority in their daily schedules and gave unstinting support to the PR team in their efforts.

Who needs whom?

Considering that they are two groups who need each other in order to get much of their work done, it's true that journalists and PR people do often struggle to get along. There's an essential tension that is caused by the constantly shifting balance of power – a classic love–hate relationship that has fault on both sides, with both parties capable of behaving badly. Journalists complain that PR people fail to get back to them, send them the wrong information, no information or badly written information, are not properly briefed on their subject, or display a lack of knowledge about the publication the journalist works for. PR people in return say that they have to deal with rude, aggressive or lazy journalists, who can get away with unreasonable behaviour because of their position of power.

However, the balance of power shifts all the time within the

PR–journalist relationship, depending on the circumstances. Madonna's PR agent, Barbara Charone, held considerable power in the build-up to the singer's 2001 'Drowned World' tour, with journalists desperate for any scrap of information they could get. She held the power and could dictate her terms to the press.

On the other hand, BBC Radio 4's flagship news programme, *Today*, holds considerable power because it is seen to set the news agenda for the day. There is enormous kudos to be had in the business world if a company succeeds in positive coverage on the programme. The journalists and researchers working on the programme, therefore, can dictate the terms under which they will run a story – terms such as whom they want to interview and at what time.

It is perhaps obvious why PR needs journalists: attempting to get your business written about favourably in the media means that you'll need to work with those whose job it is to write the stories – the journalists. But why should journalists need PR?

Journalists have to fill space – whether it be on the page, on TV, radio or the Internet, and therefore need a constant supply of good ideas to consider. So PR isn't just about 'selling' a story: it's also about fulfilling a genuine media requirement.

Journalists require reliable sources of information. Your business may be in a position to provide this, even though the journalist is not working on a story related to your company on this occasion. Good PR–journalist relationships are established between those who understand that not every phone call will lead to editorial coverage, but it is another deposit of goodwill in the bank.

Journalists often need a quick response. Often, journalists will be working close to deadline when they contact you. A PR-focused business will understand the need for a quick, efficient response – whether you are in a position to help or not.

Stargazing

The growing media obsession with celebrity has ensured that more and more people in the public eye hire PR consultants to help them manage their personal image and profile. This celebrity culture means that there is great demand for any titbit of information – the more scandalous the better – about the lives of the rich and famous. Publications such as *Hello!* and

OK! in the UK – who secure often exclusive access to celebrities and VIPs by not only offering a large fee, but also by granting them final veto over all copy and photography before it is published – have subsequently become very popular. This is a dream come true for the stars, because it gives them a high degree of control over what is being reported. However, it also means that the line between genuine editorial and paid-for publicity gets confused with traditional non-paid-for media-relations work. Some journalists are concerned that objectivity is being lost as more celebrities demand this right of veto as a matter of course.

One tabloid newspaper decided enough was enough, after it believed one too many changes had been requested by the British TV presenters Richard Madeley and Judy Finnigan to an interview they gave to the paper. The newspaper printed both versions of the interview – the paper's and the edited one approved by the TV couple – in an attempt to highlight the problem. However, celebrities can hardly be blamed for trying to influence how they are portrayed in the media, and are often the victims of stories that are just plain made up, so the tussle between the two sides is set to run and run. Playing go-between is what the PR adviser must do, while continuing to achieve the no mean feat of keeping everybody happy.

What makes news?

Journalists are always interested in news – but, as we'll see in the next section, your own view of what's news and theirs may differ. You may be excited about the latest contract your business has won, but in reality it may be of little interest to others beyond your immediate trade media, and, even then, if space is tight, it may not be used.

It's tough to be truly objective about what's happening in your own business, but it's important to strive for this when undertaking media-relations activity, so you can be realistic in your expectations. However, this doesn't mean that what you have to say isn't worth saying, just that you need to be always looking for the 'story' in whatever you present to the media.

Take a look at the following definitions of what makes news from a journalist's perspective:

Proximity

Where something happens is of particular importance. National newspapers, magazines, periodicals and the Internet usually define location in more global terms ('home' news will precede 'overseas' news unless something of international significance has happened). Regional newspapers, radio and TV stations, however, are driven by the local agenda in their immediate area because that is what sets them apart from their national counterparts.

Immediacy

When something happens is of prime importance with news. A story may have happened only yesterday, but may be classed as 'old news' by the 24-hour news channels that are reporting events as they unfold. Conversely, a monthly publication will be more tolerant of older stories, because its editorial deadlines are often three to four months in advance of the date it will go on sale.

Change

What has happened or changed is the essence of all news. News stories live or die by the strength of what this change is. For instance, a soft-drinks company may launch a new soda, but in what way is it different from its competitors? The scale of this change will be a vital element in whether its introduction to the market is simply a trade story or deserving of a national newspaper attention. News stories that run over a period of days or even weeks (such as coverage of a long-running court case or build-up to a major event) will always have some element of change happening each day that keeps the story fresh.

Prominence

Who is involved often determines the importance of the news. If a boy is caught smoking cannabis, it may receive a cursory mention on the inside pages of his local newspaper. The town's mayor doing the same thing would be unquestionably front-page news, with maybe a mention on the inside pages of a national newspaper (unless it was, say, the current London mayor, Ken Livingstone, who has a very high public profile and is therefore front-page material nationally). The same goes for celebrities and pop stars. Victoria and David Beckham need only to walk down the street and it seems to make the headlines.

Conflict

Human beings at odds with each other – wars, arguments, rows, debates, disagreements, fights, outbursts, neighbours from hell, political bun fights, you name it – always fill the news pages because of the assumption that everyone likes to read about others in some sort of conflict. The BBC TV newsreader Martyn Lewis himself became the subject of news a few years ago when he complained that there were not enough good-news stories being given airtime. While there was quite a lot of support for his view, nothing ultimately changed because bad news will always be more dramatic than good.

Sex

Any aspect of sex, whether it's titillating, horrifying, informative, absurd or just gratuitous, will attract substantial interest from readers or viewers. Page 3 of the *Sun* is the most obvious example of how sex sells newspapers, but you'll also find it in a more subtle form in the broadsheets and on television.

Suspense

Just as any self-regarding TV soap will end each episode with a cliffhanger plot line, designed to ensure you tune in tomorrow to find out what happens, news stories that cover events that have an element of suspense tap into our curiosity. Miners trapped underground following a blast, a child who falls down a well, ponies that become stuck in quicksand, firefighters battling with out-of-control fires – all of these make compelling viewing. We want to know how things will turn out.

Consumer issues

There's been a shift in general news reporting over the past ten or fifteen years towards consumer-based issues, because editorial policy-makers believe these are the types of story people are interested in. For example, cooking, gardening and DIY are enjoying huge popularity at the moment with numerous TV shows, magazines, radio programmes and newspaper supplements devoted to these subjects.

News reporting, therefore, follows suit and reflects this trend with a greater focus on related issues such as health, the environment and leisure. What should we be eating for optimum health? How much are we spending on our homes? What's happened to the common or garden sparrow to make its numbers fall so dramatically?

Emotion

Hate, anger, love, resentment, guilt, betrayal, loss, joy, hope, frustration – any extreme emotion makes compelling news, irrespective of who is experiencing it. A crowd demonstrating against a new road development, the parents making a plea to find their lost child, an athlete crying with joy at winning the gold, the family left destitute after an earthquake. Close-up interviews to catch that moment of unbridled emotion are more and more the norm in news reporting.

Oddity/uniqueness

Like change, this is about focusing on the thing that is out of the ordinary: the first, last, best, worst, longest, shortest, fattest, fastest, ugliest, most beautiful – anything that is at the extreme or is unusual will be a contender for the news pages. The smallest mobile phone, the biggest hot-air balloon, the fastest computer, the toughest yacht race in the world – businesses can hit the news jackpot if they have a genuine first to shout about.

Also in this category are landmark events such as the thousandth item off the production line, the five hundredth customer of the new restaurant, the first shopper at the new out-of-town mall.

It's easy to spot when there's not much genuine news around because you'll start to see weaker stories getting quite high-profile treatment. It's known as the 'silly season' – traditionally during the summer when Parliament is in recess and news reporters are left scrabbling around for anything they can get. This can be a good time to launch a new product, which may receive more coverage than would normally be given.

Shock, horror

Tabloid editors are constantly on the look out for stories that have a shock or surprise angle. The *Sun* specialises in running these as front-page stories such as FREDDIE STARR ATE MY HAMSTER! (light entertainer accused of dubious meal), and GOTCHA! (sinking of the

General Belgrano during the Falklands War). The aim is to get an emotional reaction out of the reader or viewer and so provoke them into buying the newspaper or staying with the channel.

Tools of the trade

PR is the dream job for those with a mind that thrives on coming up with new ideas and creative solutions to problems. The challenge of PR, and in particular the media-relations aspect of the job, is consistently to provide an interesting slant on information that on first glance may even seem dull or humdrum. In a world where the ordinary outweighs the number of genuine 'firsts', 'biggests', 'longests' and 'tallests', the job of PR is (a) to dig out the news value of what you want to say and (b) to present it in a way that carries maximum impact and interest appropriate to the audience you are trying to reach.

There are twelve basic media-relations tools that are most commonly used by PR experts, to achieve editorial coverage:

Tool 1: Press release

The press release is to the PR function what the spreadsheet is to accounting or the letter is to law. It's the most basic and most used form of communication in the PR toolbox. Even if a PR specialist will be writing it for you, you'll be the one authorising it to go out, so use these basic do's and don'ts as your checklist:

Do ...

Think news. Get the Who, What, Why and When up front – preferably in the first paragraph. You are aiming to have the crux of the story spelled out in summary at the start, so anyone picking it up can immediately grasp what it's about. Take a look at a national newspaper news story – you'll that see the main points are covered in the opening paragraph.

Think audience. Take the trouble to adapt your press release to suit the medium you are targeting and you'll increase the chances that it will at least be read by the journalist. A tabloid newspaper such as the *Sun* and a broadsheet such as the *Sunday Times* have very different styles, readerships and therefore needs, as do specialist-interest magazines that serve a particular industry such as the *Architect's Journal* and

Caterer & Hotelkeeper. It's even possible in some instances to have three or four versions of the same story, each written with a different focus and style, such as for the trade or specialist industry media, national broadsheet, tabloid and regional newspapers (which require a special local focus to the story).

Think relevance. Much as you would like to think the exciting new business win or deal should be of interest to everyone, you've got to try to view it from an outsider's perspective. If you don't know it already, take the trouble to get familiar with your key trade publications and look at the sorts of story they run – and remember to target your news to suit.

Think length. Attention spans are getting shorter. In the US, TV channel hopping is practically a national sport. In the UK, the BBC has a policy of running thirty-second 'highlights' trailers at the beginning of dramas to try to keep viewers watching. The written word can present even more of a challenge. A press release should say all it needs to on one side of A4 – with extra pages for backup material only if absolutely necessary. Don't swamp them with pages and pages of bumf. A good way to get additional information across is to include a section at the end of the release called 'Notes To Editors', which is where supporting details can go. The main objective is first to grab their attention and then provide backup information if they are interested. To do otherwise is just a waste of time and trees.

Think time. Time is usually in short supply with journalists, who will be worrying about their deadlines. Remember the Three Golden Ws and find out when they will be on deadline and aim to work around this.

Think timing. Getting the timing right for creating maximum impact for your story is a key element of a successful media-relations strategy. Holiday periods are good, such as Christmas and the summer months, when there are traditionally fewer big stories happening and your chances of getting exposure for other lower-profile stories increase. The reverse is, of course, true. At times of major conflict and disaster, such as the World Trade Center attacks in 2001 and the subsequent war in Afghanistan, all nonessential stories get knocked off the page instantly.

Think follow-up. Remember that one of the responsibilities of PR is to help make a journalist's life easy, so contact details for more information should be prominent on the release, with preferably *two* contacts listed in case one is not available.

Think accuracy. A basic point, but any release that includes factual errors, spelling mistakes or grammatical errors deserves to be put straight in the bin – and probably will be!

Don't ...

Get disheartened. Out of the thousands of press releases sent out every day, only a small proportion will actually get used – especially by the national media. However, don't be discouraged: just work hard at ensuring yours are well thought out, accurately targeted and appropriately delivered. PR has a wonderful way of delivering exactly what you want, just when you think it's never going to happen. Sometimes serendipity steps in, too.

Iain Munro runs Wheel Time, which renovates and hires out classic cars, and had been trying to attract media interest for a while. Then he got his big break. A mainstream men's lifestyle magazine was looking around for a good double-page feature after being let down on one they had planned to run. With only a few days before deadline, they contacted Munro's business. The magazine had found out about Wheel Time through the various press releases Munro had sent to it over the previous year, although so far they had not been able to use any of the information. The resulting feature resulted in floods of phone calls from interested potential customers and a subsequent uplift in business.

Abdicate responsibility. If you're working with a PR consultancy or in-house expert, make sure they have the right information and support to do the job. I've worked with several clients who assumed that, after they had briefed us as to what they wanted (usually lots of editorial coverage), they assumed their involvement and responsibility for the outcome was over. Not so. If your press release does create interest, the journalist will usually be looking for a brief conversation with somebody senior, preferably the MD of the business, which means making yourself available to meet their deadline.

Many times, we had interest from a journalist, but an MD who just didn't make it a priority to call them back, so missing deadline – and the editorial coverage.

Tool 2: Photographs

The saying 'a picture is worth a thousand words' is never more relevant than when it comes to photographs in the media. Most publications will have someone specifically in charge of selecting or commissioning photography – either a picture editor on a national or regional newspaper, or the art editor or production editor on a magazine. Whether you can get a picture to work for you depends once again on knowing whom you are targeting and what their needs are. Different publications like different pictures – and each style of photography will dictate the type of photographer you need to work with to get the desired results.

Take a few minutes to flick through some publications and observe what sorts of photograph they are using. If it's a technical publication, then there will probably be product shots. If it's a news-based title, then people shots will be prevalent. Consumer magazines include a mix of both. Often, magazines will develop their own 'house style' for photographs that contribute to its particular brand image.

The use of photography in PR can be very effective, if the picture is taken with a specific audience or type of publication in mind and with some creative thinking about the shot.

Big shots in the City

A good example of creative photography at work can often be seen in the City and business pages of the quality daily newspapers. A photograph is used to liven up the page and provide a 'people' focus to an otherwise rather dry financial story. The juxtaposing of a CEO with their company's product is a popular shot – perhaps sitting in the driver's cab of one of his fleet of buses or next to racks of clothes in a warehouse. British Airways had particular success with a City-pages picture story when it announced the launch of its business and first-class passenger arrivals lounge. Peter Jones, who was head of corporate communications for British Airways at the time, explains, 'We managed to persuade Bob Ayling, then chief executive of BA, to pose holding a razor and just a towel wrapped around his waist. The shot was a great success because it was both striking and relevant. A great picture that told our story in one.'

Case study: Picture power

The impact of photographs can be profound. They transcend language, stay in our mind's eye and have the ability to affect our behaviour and influence opinion. In the middle of the foot-and-mouth crisis in the UK in 2001, a picture was taken of the British Prime Minister, Tony Blair, wearing a yellow protective jacket as he visited an area of suspected outbreak. The photograph was flashed around the world and thousands of overseas tourists planning to visit on holiday were said to cancel their bookings as a result.

Even though the disease posed no threat to humans and the Prime Minster was simply adhering to standard health-and-safety practices by wearing the jacket, it unfortunately gave out the message, 'Britain is unsafe'. The crisis was one that was particularly defined by photographs: whether they were of piles of burning cattle or Phoenix the calf, saved from slaughter at the eleventh hour by a government keen to appease public opinion, pictures told a story more powerfully than words ever could.

Photocalls

A far riskier strategy than actually supplying the photograph yourself, is to invite the media to attend a 'photo opportunity', which is known as the photocall. This tool is best used if you are working with a celebrity or VIP, who has the power to attract the media's attention in their own right, which is why they are being used in the first place. It is high-risk, though, because it relies on having many factors in place on the day: (1) that there is no other bigger story running or breaking at the time of your photocall, because, if there is, photographers will be diverted by their news and picture editors to the more newsworthy story; (2) that it isn't pouring with rain, which would make for difficult conditions for taking photographs; (3) that the picture editors like your idea and remember to put it in the diary for that day's schedule; (4) and that the photographer actually turns up!

Even if everything is in place, there's still no guarantee that a picture taken at the photocall will be used. So the photocall is a tactic that takes a huge amount of effort and should be attempted only if you are pretty confident of success. Even then, something bigger can happen in the news agenda and knock your story off the page. It's a great tactic to use if it comes off, but, if for any reason it doesn't, be sure you're prepared to risk the cost of setting it up.

Tool 3: Features

Features differ from news stories in that they look at a subject in more depth. They can be used to provide background to a particular news item, or simply to look at a topic in more detail. They are also less time-sensitive than straight news stories. Many magazines and some newspapers make information on planned features available to businesses. These 'Forward Features' lists, together with media packs giving circulation and target reader information, can be obtained by contacting the advertising or editorial departments.

There are four main types of 'feature' used in the media:

a. Regular topic-based features

Newspapers carry regular feature sections on popular areas of interest to their readership, such as gardening, cookery, travel, health and education. The pieces are generated by the publication itself, but do often rely on PR-generated material to contribute to the feature.

Specialist industry publications and programmes often use features to take the 'pulse' of what's available in a particular market. So, for example, if your business is in the dairy food sector, then it's important to know when the next in-depth look at yoghurt, butter or milk will be, so you can make sure you provide the magazine with the latest information about your products. Most publications of this type produce 'forward features listings' which detail the planned features for the next six to twelve months.

b. People-based features

These are usually profiles of personalities, celebrities and people in the public eye, and are popular in national newspapers and consumer magazines. Specialist industry publications also run people-based features, which may be in the form of 'opinion' pieces or straight profiles.

You don't have to be Mick Jagger to get a profile piece, but you do need something relevant and interesting to say. If your business is doing something unusual or is particularly successful, or one of the senior management team has an interesting track record, then this type of approach could work for your business.

c. Prepared features

These have been written by either a PR expert or freelance journalist and can be submitted to a newspaper, magazine or business journal for consideration. However, the piece needs to be impartial, providing expert advice, say, but not flogging a particular product or service. That's simply advertising. For example, if you are running a management consultancy, you may consider submitting a piece to a relevant business publication on successful recruitment strategies. The feature wouldn't talk about how wonderful your particular consultancy is, but about the latest ideas and industry trends on hiring and keeping employees. You could use a few examples of your own direct experience, but, overall, you are offering impartial advice.

If you stray into plugging your own business, the feature loses credibility instantly and will probably not be used. The benefit to a business of supplying such a piece is for the credit or name check at the end of the article and the expert status it will afford you, thereby building up your profile with the reader and also with the publication itself, which may come back to you for more if the piece is good.

d. Advertising-led features

This tactic is used often in regional newspapers, which may, for example, run a feature on 'eating alfresco this summer' and then approach local restaurants to advertise alongside the piece. The newspaper will usually promise to include an 'editorial' piece about your business if you advertise.

It can be useful exposure, providing you with total control over what the article says about your company, but bear in mind that this is advertising-led, so the impact on the readers may be less than a genuine piece of non-paid-for, objective editorial.

Tool 4: Case studies

Case studies are a great way to demonstrate your product or service in action and provide your story with the all-important 'people' focus that the media are always looking for. They work particularly well in trade and specialist industry publications, because this type of medium is interested in providing help and guidance for its readership. By using case studies either produced by its own editorial team or supplied unsolicited by a business operating in its area of interest, the publication can highlight a relevant issue or topic. Case studies work on three basic levels:

1. Credibility

Case studies provide *credibility* to your message. It's no good merely saying that lots of customers think your product/service is the best. PR is all about getting others to say it for you. The case study provides the perfect format for this.

2. People

Case studies focus on *people*. People stories sell newspapers and magazines and attract viewers and listeners to TV, radio and the Internet. The media are therefore naturally very keen on them.

During the course of the second series of the UK's Channel 4 *Big Brother* programme, 15.5 million votes were cast by the public – more than for any single political party during the 2001 British general election. The tabloid media ran almost blanket coverage of the personalities involved in the show and sold millions of extra copies as a result. By including people stories in your PR, you may not achieve quite this scale of success, but you will be keeping in step with what the media are increasingly focused on.

3. Long life

Case studies have *longevity*. Where news is always time-sensitive, case studies and features are less so, which means they will have a longer shelf life than press releases. Building a library of case studies provides a solid source of reference. You may choose to give them out to potential customers as sales tools or reproduce them in employee or customer newsletters.

The great thing about case studies is that, once they are prepared, they provide a record and snapshot of achievement that may otherwise be forgotten as you get caught up in the next big challenge facing your business.

Bringing your story to life

For many years, ABC worked for Berkhamsted-based Prologic Computer Consultants. The company specialises in providing comprehensive management information systems to the fashion industry. Our job was to achieve editorial exposure for Prologic across its core target medium, the fashion trade press. One of the main problems we faced in meeting this objective was that the target medium was not very interested in writing about computers. Understandably perhaps, it preferred pictures and stories that were full of fashion type images and news.

However, we made the point that any company operating in the fashion industry still had to worry about normal business issues such as premises, accounting, recruitment and, of course, computer systems. To illustrate our argument, we began supplying the magazines with case studies of Prologic customers whose businesses had been supported and, in some cases, transformed by installing and using their management information computer system. Customers such as Paul Smith, Mulberry and Dune agreed to participate in the case studies because it also made good sense from their own publicity point of view. The result was a win–win–win situation. Our client achieved good editorial coverage, which featured third-party endorsement in their target publications; their clients also received positive editorial exposure in publications that were relevant to their own businesses; and the magazines themselves had good copy that filled space and provided interesting and pertinent information to their readership.

Tool 5: Advertorials

Advertorials inhabit a sort of no-man's-land between PR and advertising. They are bought and paid for as an advertisement is, but can be written either by the editorial team or PR specialists and have the 'look and feel' of genuine editorial in the publication. They are used as a PR tool when guaranteed exposure is required. Magazines generally love them because they are great money spinners, and PR consultancies like them because it is one area of media relations where they can actually guarantee that coverage will appear in a particular target publication.

Cynics will say that advertorials are there simply to dupe the reader into believing they are being offered impartial editorial. Even though all advertorials will display somewhere on the page the words 'advertorial' or 'promotion', the fact that the space has been paid for is not always obvious to the reader.

However, advertorials do have their place in the PR toolbox and can provide businesses with an opportunity to gain vital exposure exactly when and where they need it.

When PR is paid for
There is a growing trend among specialist trade publications
and periodicals for what is called 'colour-separation charges'. A
magazine will run a picture alongside a story only if a charge is
paid for the processing of the picture. Some publications won't
even run the story if the charge is not paid. This is a really
sneaky practice, because it is effectively charging for advertising
by the back door. There are moves currently in the UK PR
industry to flush the practice into the open by lobbying the
Periodical Publishers' Association (the official body of the magazine industry) to force publishers to display the words 'advertisement' or 'promotion' next to any editorial or photograph
that has been paid for in this way.

In truth, the practice puts many businesses in a difficult position if the number of titles serving their particular target market
is restricted to those that use this advertising-by-stealth system.
A client of ABC's was in just this position. Its main trade title
operated a colour separation charge system on its 'editorial'
pages. Our client had little option but to go ahead and pay the
fees if it wanted information about its products to appear. We
argued that if the story carried strong news value, and it was
therefore appropriate for a picture of the product to appear
alongside the story, it should run without the charge. The magazine disagreed and the client had to cough up or face seeing the
story dropped.

Tool 6: Competitions and promotions

From the ubiquitous 'win a car' promotion to the elaborate
'Dungeons & Dragons'-style puzzles that have to be solved before
you can collect your prize, we are bombarded every day with chances
to have something for nothing. Or at least in exchange for allowing
our details to be entered into someone's database. Companies use
competitions because they are an ideal vehicle for promoting their
product or service in a rather more exciting way than straight advertising.

Usually run under the editorial banner and managed within the context of PR activity, competitions, if planned and executed well, have the ability to engage an audience because they demand participation. Competitions and promotions are also popular with publishers and producers because, by offering a competition idea to them, you are also contributing to the appeal of that publication, radio show or TV programme, which in turn is good for its own business.

Promotions are slightly different from competitions in that they tend to run over a period of time, often requiring readers to collect tokens, thus encouraging repeated purchase of the publication and offering the company extended publicity in each issue. These types of offer, such as two-for-one meals and reduced-price flight tickets, are often self-financing, as, once in receipt of the discounted product on offer, the consumer can usually be expected to buy more, or repeat-purchase if the experience has been a good one.

If you do decide to run a competition or promotion, take a look first at some basic rules:

- **Do** work out what your overall objective is from the outset. Is it a data-capturing exercise, a way of building interest in a new product or brand loyalty? Whatever the reason, remember to take note of the position you're starting from, so you'll know if your actions have made a difference. What are the criteria for evaluating whether the activity has been a success?

- **Do** work out whether you want to go for quantity or quality if it's a database you're building. A specialist-interest publication may offer you a smaller number of potential targets, but the readership will at least have a proven interest in the subject. For example, a snowboard manufacturer may choose to run a competition in a specialist snowboarding magazine or a wider-interest magazine such as *FHM*. The general-interest magazine will have a much higher circulation, but not everyone reading it will necessarily be into snowboards, so the effectiveness of the promotion may be reduced.

- **Don't** forget that to gain new names and addresses for a database for direct-mail purposes in the UK, you must comply with the new Data Protection Act of 1998, which came into force on 1 March 2000. Essentially, data subjects have to 'consent' to receive further communication and silence cannot be taken to mean acceptance. The new law applies to anyone processing personal information, whether they are paper records or those held on computer. Everyone must register with the Data Commissioner and adhere to the eight principles laid out in the new Act. Useful websites to look at are: the Data Protection Commissioner (www.dataprotection.gov.uk); the Mail preference website, if you are going to send any direct mail (www.mpsonline.org.uk).

■ **Don't** underestimate the response. We ran many competitions on behalf of clients over the years and, if our office address was used for the responses, Ray the postman would curse us as he lugged yet another bulging sackful through the door. Many publications or broadcast programmes usually deal with the response-handling themselves so that they can control the data, so agree upfront who will be responsible for this. If you're keen to keep the data, you may have to deal with this yourself – or get your PR consultancy to do it for you!

■ **Don't** forget to keep to the official rules for competitions and promotions and always check you can fulfil what you are promising. A great idea can turn into a full-blown PR disaster when someone forgets to check the small print or makes promises that just can't be delivered. The Hoover 'free flights to America' promotion in 1992 famously came to grief when it was revealed that the company hadn't done its research properly. Consumers were promised two free flights to the US if they spent more than £250 on Hoover products. Research by this home-appliance manufacturer suggested that they could expect around 50,000 responses. However, Hoover were staggered to receive more than 200,000 and simply couldn't meet the demand. They quickly became embroiled in a very public row with demands for compensation and threats of legal action from upset customers. The company never fully recovered and their European division was sold off in 1995 as a result. Guidance on competition and promotional rules can be found by contacting the Institute of Sales Promotion (www.isp.org.uk).

Tool 7: Launch events, press conferences and press trips

The PR launch is easily the most overused and abused activity in the PR armoury. Visions of *Absolutely Fabulous*-type PR luvvies swanning around, sipping champagne and not doing much else is the stereotype, and I'm afraid to say that in some cases it is also the reality. While PR will probably never shake off its share of schmoozers and boozers, there's no reason to let this rather depressing image put you off the brilliant benefits to be had from a properly organised, well-targeted, focused PR 'event', run by people who know what they are doing. If you are sure it will fulfil a clear and serious objective, then by all means go for it.

Tanya Lake, MD of the consultancy Red Rooster Consumer & Beauty PR in London, has hosted many PR events for clients over the years and believes an event's success lies in good planning and knowing what you're doing it for. 'We organised the launch party for *Sports Illustrated* magazine's entry into the UK market during 2000,' she says. 'Right from the start, we sat down with them to find out exactly what their expectations were for the event, such as how many guests did they want there, which type of guests did we need to attract (buyers, journalists, celebrities etcetera), did they expect editorial coverage as a result and so on.'

The event proved to be a great success, with Red Rooster able to focus on getting the right people to attend and the client happy because expectations were clear from the start and were then met. Press coverage is sometimes the main objective for a launch party – for a new drink, say – so that there's an opportunity for the paparazzi to photograph someone famous with it, such as a well-known champagne brand achieved when a few top models were pictured sipping its demi-bottle drink through straws.

However, it's just not possible or appropriate for everyone to have such glamorous guests attend. Sometimes, launch parties are simply about getting a few crucial people, such as potential customers or existing buyers, to meet the senior management in a relaxed and informal situation.

Press conferences are a more regimented form of event and ideal for announcements of major importance. As a formal briefing session that is designed to cater for the needs of the media, the press conference gives senior company executives the platform to communicate with journalists in a direct and controlled way. Journalists are provided with the opportunity to pose questions and all receive the same information at the same time – an important consideration in the highly competitive world of journalism.

However, press conferences are to be used only when the story is strong enough to warrant them. Journalists have little time to spare and will not appreciate being dragged out to a conference where there is little news value. Press conferences are more common with publicly quoted companies that have financial results or acquisitions to announce. For the smaller business, informal receptions or briefings where there is an opportunity to talk on a one-to-one basis are usually more appropriate.

Press trips can also be an excellent way to provide journalists with first hand experience of the products/environment/personnel relevant to the story in question. For example, Midnight Communications organised such a trip on behalf of Adobe Systems Inc., where a select group of senior journalists visited Adobe's headquarters in San Francisco to attend the launch of the company's new business strategy. In addition, one-to-one interviews were organised with several of the Adobe Systems senior management team and several in-depth articles appeared across Adobe's target media as a result. However, be careful to ensure, when considering a press trip, that there is indeed real news and benefit on offer. Freebie junkets just for the hell of it may win you friends in the short term, but, if you want to keep credibility, keep it relevant.

Tool 8: Attention grabbers and stunts

Journalists receive a mountain of information every day by post, telephone, fax and now email. Of prime importance, therefore, is to put some thought into making your contribution to this avalanche stand out from the rest. Otherwise, it's like turning up to a fancy-dress party only to find that everyone else thought that going as King Kong would be funny too.

Whole industries, of course, are dedicated to grabbing the attention. Direct-marketing and advertising agencies devote much of their creative firepower to coming up with ways to do precisely this on behalf of their clients. Often in PR, the most important thing you can do is to make sure that you're being listened to, so you at least have the chance to persuade the journalist that your information is worth looking at.

At ABC, we often used attention grabbers (or 'teasers') when approaching the media on behalf of our clients. Whether it was sending handwritten 'wish-you-were-here'-style postcards promoting a city's new website or brown paper bags inviting journalists to use them if they were having a bad-hair day (we were promoting hair-care products), our attention grabbers did just that. Not only were they noticed by the majority of people we wanted to reach, but they also gave us an all-important first conversation piece.

Invitations to launches, events and parties can be a crucial factor in encouraging attendance, so are important attention grabbers in their own right. Making them an unusual size, colour or shape dramatically reduces the chance they'll be lost in the deluge of other mail.

When it comes to getting others to take notice, however, it's the PR stunt that really has the potential to take the biscuit. Often, those most successful also are at most risk from backfiring – but it's that element of danger that often makes them work. Cadbury's projection of its Whisper chocolate brand on to the domed Whispering Gallery of St Paul's Cathedral was a particularly audacious stunt that attracted uproar from the church at the time, but resulted in acres of national newspaper coverage for the brand. easyJet must be a contender for the Sheer Cheek Award of the Year, when it booked ten seats on the inaugural flight of its rival low-cost flight operator Go and filled them with liveried easyJet staff, who proceeded to hand out easyJet promotional material to Go passengers.

Some industries are more used to PR stunts than others, such as those in the entertainment world. Here, dreaming up crazy ways of getting noticed can be a regular part of the PR job. Judd Lander, one of the most experienced PR men in the music business, became well known for his madcap stunts and willingness to go beyond the call of duty when it came to grabbing attention.

'I once was trying to get a single playlisted by the BBC's Radio One,' says Lander, 'and missed a crucial meeting with two of the producers whose job it was to choose that week's singles. So I decided something drastic was called for.'

The planning meeting was held on the fifth floor of the BBC building, so Lander arranged for a helium balloon to float him up to the level of the executives' open window just as they were in discussion, so he could lob in copies of the single. Crazy, undoubtedly, and definitely not recommended – but the single did make it onto the playlist the following week!

Stunts that go wrong, though, do tend to hang around to haunt the perpetrators for some time afterwards. One chief executive was persuaded to pose for a photograph with a hard hat on, while pushing a vacuum cleaner. I'm not sure what the reason was for the original stunt, but, every time the chief executive was quoted in the trade media thereafter, there would be that picture, making him look ludicrous, no matter what the context of his quote was.

Stunt do's and don'ts

- **Do** always make sure that there is a solid news link to the planned stunt. Be clear about why you are doing the stunt and what you aim to get from it.

- **Do** be careful to avoid getting carried away with the idea. Think through the practicalities – if it's outside, for example, what happens if it's raining? Avoid using animals as props: they tend to do the unexpected.

- **Don't** rely on newspaper photographers or TV film crews turning up, just because they said they would. Book your own photographer, or even film crew if necessary, to ensure you have your own record of the event.

- **Do** be wary when booking celebrities/VIPs/politicians – double check the booking and keep in contact with their agent or assistant to minimise the risk of a no-show.

- **Do** remember that the results from stunts are highly unpredictable. It's a gamble, so be prepared for it not to work out as you planned.

- **Don't** forget that stunts that go wrong can stick around in the collective memory and filing cabinets of the media for some time to come. So be prepared to live with the consequences!

Tool 9: Surveys

How many times a week do you eat breakfast? Are you one of the 36 per cent of people who sometimes eat breakfast or one of the 52 per cent who just grab a cup of tea or coffee to set them up for the day? Perhaps you are in the 7 per cent who always sit down to the full works or even the 3 per cent who don't know/can't say/won't say what they do? (Those are fake stats, by the way, but serve to make the point.)

As humans, we are very interested in how we fit into our society. Do we conform or are we a bit of an odd bod? The popularity of surveys in the media shows our insatiable desire for statistics about how we and others behave, think and act. In fact, there's a saying that, next to hard news, surveys gain the most media attention. It's not hard to see that surveys are indeed very popular with both the journalists who use the stories and their readers, listeners and viewers, who like reading and hearing about them.

If a major part of the skill of PR is providing the media with the information that they want, then it's no wonder that providing good, interesting, statistically sound surveys is one of the most popular PR tools around.

Take a look at today's newspapers. It's a safe bet that in at least one if not more there will be a survey, revealing some hitherto uncovered quirk, attitude, behaviour or trend, such as (and these figures are for illustration only, too) that three out of five people now eat their evening meal in front of the telly; that 60 per cent of 18–22-year-olds would rather listen to music than have a conversation with their parents; that 25 per cent of the world's forests will be wiped out by the year 2005. But, if you are the company that has produced the research, what's the benefit to you?

The answer is twofold: first, it is a simple tactic to achieve editorial coverage, while providing information that has a credible link to your business/product/service, and thus raising profile. Secondly, surveys have the potential to deliver greater benefits to a business than a simple media-relations exercise, by producing useful data that can be used across the sales, marketing and R&D functions.

Nescafé, the UK's best-selling coffee brand, conducted a survey into whether the line 'Do you want to come in for a coffee?' after a date was actually a sincere offer of a late-night cuppa, or a euphemism for something else. The results were not only amusing, but gained the coffee giant good coverage in the media. The skill was to identify a topic that struck a chord with lots of people, was humorous and provided a strong link between popular-coffee drinking habits and the Nescafé brand.

Survey do's and don'ts

■ **Do** be clear from the outset why you are conducting the survey. If it is purely to gain editorial coverage then remember that, as with all other PR-initiated editorial information, there are no absolute guarantees that the results will get used. Another point to bear in mind is that, although the data may get used, your company's name may well be edited out of the story. Very frustrating and not particularly fair, but some journalists will do this if they think the survey endorses your company too strongly. One way around this is, before going ahead, to offer exclusivity to one publication in return for a guarantee that they will run the results and provide you with a credit. Bear in mind, however, that this does restrict the number of people who will get to see it.

- **Do** consider the cost. Prices range from around $3,000 to more than $22,000. If you are working with a PR specialist, they should be able to recommend to you a suitable research company who will conduct the survey. If not, take a look at the British Market Research Association's (BMRA) website (www.bmra.org.uk/ selectline), which lists more than two hundred BMRA members, together with advice on how to choose the right research agency for you.

- **Do** give careful consideration to timing. Is there a particular event about to happen with which you can time your survey results? Perhaps an industry exhibition where your survey will give you something different to talk about. Also, the chances of getting your information used are greater during traditionally quieter times for the media, such as the school summer holidays and the period just after Christmas, when they are on the lookout for stories.

- **Don't** forget that a survey can have 'legs'. By having legs I mean the ability to run and gain a momentum of its own. The data you uncover may provide invaluable insights into the behaviour and attitudes of your target customers, which you can then use in your sales and marketing activities. You could use the results in newsletters, presentations and brochures. Also, if you conduct surveys on a regular basis, you will have a way of comparing how things are changing over a period of time.

Tool 10: The lunch

The PR lunch suffers from a rather dodgy reputation, but it is a valuable PR tool nonetheless. Its overuse, however, is not recommended. First, because many journalists simply do not have the time to spare (reductions in staffing levels across many areas of the media have meant increased pressure on those remaining). Secondly, you can communicate what you need to very effectively – and usually more efficiently for the journalist – by simply sticking to the Three Golden Ws and giving them the information in a timely, appropriate and efficient way.

However, that said, because a key function of PR is to build positive, ongoing relationships with those with whom you must communicate, there's nothing quite like meeting someone face to face. This is particularly true in the area of trade or business-to-business PR, where journalists view meeting businesses in their area of interest as an important part of the job. The lunch or dinner appointment offers a more relaxed and informal opportunity for discussion, where understanding can be gained and information provided.

Spending the time to build a few synergic relationships with key journalists in this way makes sound business sense. Remember, though, that, however friendly your contacts may be, they are still journalists first and are there to do a job. Providing background information can be helpful, but don't be too eager to reveal any information that you wouldn't be happy seeing in print.

Tool 11: Video news releases

The video news release (or VNR) is a tool used by companies to gain TV and online broadcast coverage for their business, products or services. Increasingly referred to as 'multimedia content' provision, the idea is to provide broadcast 'footage' (in the form of a broadcast-quality videotape) that features information you would like used, in a format and style that is suitable to the needs of the broadcaster. Although there is a growing industry dedicated to providing such footage, broadcasters are reluctant to admit that they use this type of material, because they fear it may compromise editorial integrity.

However, VNRs (or 'multimedia content') do still get used often and tend to work best when they are unedited, raw pieces of footage that the broadcaster can then adapt and edit to suit their own programming style. The key point is to make it easy for the broadcaster to use your material and cover your story when they may not have the resources to do otherwise.

According to the Independent Television Commission, 70 per cent of UK citizens choose TV as their preferred source of world news. With the proliferation of channels that collectively have hundreds of hours a day to fill, there is a steady growth in companies who specialise in packaging 'broadcast footage' for TV stations and online channels to use.

Case study: Putting it on a plate

The IT service company ICL achieved an audience reach of over 6 million by providing a short VNR demonstrating how its scanning machine was being used to process information from the 2001 UK population census. Although media interest in the census was considerable, broadcasters would not have had the resources or time to travel to film the machine themselves for what was, on the face of it, a fairly dry, technical story.

However, by providing all of the footage on a plate and by timing its story to provide broadcasters with an interesting angle for their census stories, ICL ensured that its scanning-machine story appeared on at least eleven TV stations – in some cases more than once.

Tool 12: Sponsorship

Although not strictly just a PR tool, sponsorship often comes under the umbrella of PR. It is really a marketing medium in its own right and demands its own focus. It is fused with PR because it undertakes to communicate information and positioning about a business or brand by creating a partnership or association with a third party, in order to reach a specific target audience. In comparison, advertising takes a more simplistic approach, where the relationship is directly between the advertiser and its target audiences (see Figure 1).

Used by businesses to deliver commercial benefits by creating or funding an appropriate vehicle, such as an event or cause, sponsorship provides benefits to both sponsor and sponsored. However, the scope of sponsorship is enormous and, like PR, means different things to different people. At one end of the scale there are charity-based sponsorships such as the Flora London Marathon (one of the highest-recalled sponsorships). At the other end are art, sport and entertainment sponsorship such as the Booker Prize for literature, Lloyds TSB's Five Nations Rugby and Britannia Music's Brit Awards (currently sponsored by Mastercard).

Successful sponsorship programmes can build powerful links that remain long after the association has finished. Who can think of

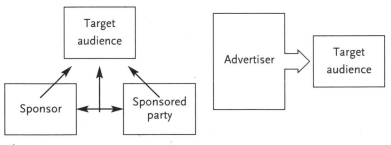

Figure 1

English test cricket without thinking of Cornhill Insurance, its sponsor of more than twenty years? Or the Premier League without thinking of Carling? Both sponsorships have now ended but, for the time being at least, remain in the common consciousness. Big or small, sponsorship can provide an excellent opportunity for a business to increase awareness and develop customer loyalty.

Katy Thomas, a sponsorship specialist of twenty years and ex-director of the leading London sponsorship agency Karen Earl Ltd, says creating a relevant association between the sponsor and the sponsored party is key. 'For sponsorship to really work, there needs to be a synergy between the sponsor and the sponsored,' she says. 'For example, NTL did a great job with its sponsorship of ITV's *Who Wants To Be a Millionaire?* quiz programme, by using the trailers before and after each commercial break to create a clever link between its technology and communication solutions and the catchphrases from the show.' Sometimes however, sheer longevity can win out: Cornhill and cricket, for example – not an obvious link, but one that endured over many years.

If you embark on sponsorship, whether it's of Wembley Stadium or the local business club, bear in mind the following golden rules:

Sponsorship secrets

Does it fit? Ensure what you sponsor provides a good fit with your image. It's hard to see why McDonald's decided to sponsor one of the PGA Championship USA events. The golfing fraternity may be a target audience for the fast-food chain, but the leap is maybe too ambitious to make in one go. Sponsorships that are the most successful are the ones where there is a logical link between the sponsor and the sponsored, such as the Red Bull energy drink and mountain-biking events.

Timing. Consider how the sponsorship will fit with your other marketing activities. Can you increase its effectiveness by dovetailing advertising, PR and direct-mail campaigns?

Geography. Bear in mind where the sponsorship will be happening. If your customers are mainly local to your city or immediate area, concentrate on sponsorship opportunities that will deliver your message to these audiences. If it is an event, ask for as much data as possible on attendees or expected visitors, so you can be sure they match whom you are trying to reach.

Measure it. Businesses often don't attempt to evaluate their sponsorship activities. Even larger corporations who invest millions in major sponsorship programmes don't bother to undertake research that will demonstrate the effectiveness of their programmes. Set out from the start the business objectives for the sponsorship and decide how you will measure whether it has achieved them. The smaller the sponsorship, the harder you will have to work to make sure your business is associated with it and that you are getting best value for money.

Resource it. It's easy to overlook the other costs associated with sponsorship programmes, such as administration, promotion and PR. To get the best from sponsorship it is rarely enough just to pay your money and sit back. Consider what else you may need to do to make it really work for you.

Media appeal. Does it have a strong news value attached? Some sponsorships, such as the Booker Prize for literature, will generate automatic media interest, but the majority will require extra effort to work up angles that will appeal to the press.

The media interview

If you incorporate PR into your business thinking and actively seek to communicate with your target audiences by working with the media, then chances are that at some point you'll find yourself in a formal media interview situation. Unfortunately for many, on the least-favourite-thing-to-do list, it ranks right up there with visits to dentist, moving house and sitting exams.

The good news is that all of these (with perhaps the exception of dental situations, where the less you think about them beforehand the better) become less scary with good preparation. As with public speaking, there are a few people who are simply born to excel in media interviews, but for most of us it's a skill that has to be learned. Take a look at the following tips to bear in mind.

Interview heaven or hell? Ten ways to get it right

1. **Define your objective**. Know why you want to take part in the interview. If you've been asked to do one by a journalist, make sure you know why it makes sense for you to say yes.
2. **Determine your key messages**. Prepare a series of points that

you want to get across during the interview and then stick to them.

3. **Keep it simple.** Repeat any important points and use simple-to-understand examples or anecdotes to illustrate what you mean. Avoid jargon and don't express 'off-the-cuff' original thought – stick to your planned messages.

4. **Use the sound of silence.** Let silence be your friend. As with negotiation tactics, less can often mean more in some interview situations. Give yourself time to think and don't be tempted just to babble on to fill the space – you'll be drawn into saying something you didn't intend to.

5. **Bridge it together.** Bridging phrases help you to sound in control and give you the opportunity to lead into one of the messages you want to communicate, for example, 'The real issue is . . .', 'People need to know . . .', 'What I can tell you is . . .', ' Our view today at XYZ . . .'

6. **Respond to questions.** It's tempting just to ignore a difficult or awkward question, but good journalists are not likely to let you get away with it. Jeremy Paxman famously asked the then UK Home Secretary, Michael Howard, the same question fourteen times during a live television interview in a bid to stop the politician from dodging a particularly tricky issue. Acknowledge the question, then 'bridge' on to one of the key messages you want to make.

7. **The 3Ts: Tell The Truth.** Don't lie. You don't need to and you will be found out, anyway. If you can't say something, explain why, but respect corporate and individual confidentiality.

8. **Anticipate the question from hell.** Good preparation before the interview will mean that you will have already considered what the worst possible question you could be asked is – and have prepared your response. Don't be caught out – if you'd really rather not talk about something, you can bet an interviewer will have it on their list!

9. **Don't shoot the messenger.** Remember that journalists are just doing their job. They need to fill column centimetres or air time and are usually on a tight deadline. Remember, however, that a media interview is never, ever just a friendly 'chat', so treat it with plenty of respect.

10. **Know the context**. If you are being invited to join a debate, or others will also be interviewed alongside you, ensure you know who they are and where they are from. Chances are there will be someone who holds an opposing view to yours, such as a competitor, lobbyist or consumer group representative. Also, bear in mind the likely style of the interview. Is it news-focused, as would be the case with BBC Radio 4's *Today* programme, or a softer, magazine format such as *GMTV* or *Lorraine Live*?

Steve Ellis, who was a journalist for twenty years, is now a leading expert in training people how to cope with media interview situations. His company, MediaAble Ltd, has trained thousands of people around the world in what to say, how to say it and when to say it – often in times of crisis. Ellis has counselled CEOs, MDs, directors, sports personalities, even broadcasters and newspaper editors themselves on how to handle media interview situations. 'A good spokesperson needs to make the "C" grade,' Ellis explains. 'This means they must have Clarity, Competence, Confidence, Control, Concern, Commitment, Consistency and, ideally, Charisma – although, unfortunately of course, not everyone will have this last one.'

If you're working with a PR consultancy, it's part of their job to steer you through the whole media-handling issue. If you're not, then see the tips in Step Six on how to handle the media yourself. In all cases, make sure you are happy with what is being proposed – and then do your homework. You wouldn't go to the bank manager unprepared to answer his or her questions on finance, so don't go into a media interview without knowing what it is you want to say and how to say it.

My own experience of working with clients in this way is that rarely do they consider spending money on formal media training unless I can scare them enough into doing so! Given that reputations take years to build, yet only moments to destroy, it's hard to see why businesses take the risk of being unprepared.

Here are a few more essential do's and don'ts:

 Don't panic. Doing it the *Dad's Army* way won't get you very far. A media interview is a great opportunity for the prepared. It is only a threat for the unprepared.

- **Don't** say something that you're not prepared to see in print. 'Off the record' is a widely discredited practice, so be careful. There's no harm in providing background information, but assume that, if you've said it, it is *on* the record.

- **Do** keep a positive attitude. Being on the defensive will only encourage the interviewer to probe more and you'll come across as shifty.

- **Do** repeat yourself. Getting your key messages across is the reason you are doing the interview, so don't be afraid to repeat one or two things if there is time.

Step Three summary

- Use PR to take advantage of the non-stop media machine, but remember you reap what you sow when it comes to building relations with journalists.

- Adopt a 'you-win-some-you-lose-some' mentality to editorial coverage, but work hard at getting the basic Three Ws right every time and see your success rate increase.

- Choosing the right PR tools for your business is key to a successful campaign. Although specialists may be putting these into practice on your behalf, the more you understand, the better you'll be able to direct the action.

Step Four – Getting What You Want from PR

Section One: PR consultancies and PR freelancers – how to choose the right one and achieve a successful partnership

The relationship that a business has with its PR consultancy or freelance PR person is one of the most important factors in the overall success of the PR activity itself. If the relationship is not functioning properly, then no matter how much money, effort or pressure is brought to bear, you will ultimately fall short of achieving all that is possible from PR. Because so much of PR is about developing relationships – with the media, with employees, with stakeholders of all kinds – then leaving yourself out of this equation doesn't make much sense.

Chemistry is a key element often underrated or overlooked by businesses when considering buying in PR expertise, whether it be a consultancy team or individual. It's a basic point, but in the business world such things are often brushed aside. Liz Lowe, brand PR manager for Coca-Cola Great Britain, believes that it's a crucial factor when you're looking for the right consultancy with which to work: 'Personal chemistry can make an enormous difference to the effectiveness of the relationship. If you trust the people, get along easily with them and are effectively working on the same wavelength, then you've already half cracked it.'

Ideas, skill and expertise are of course equally important, but there's something special about working with a team of people who really click together. The matching of mindsets is a serious point to consider. I've worked with companies where the chemistry has been spot on and a really productive relationship ensued. We also had a couple of instances where, despite best efforts, we just didn't gel. Sometimes it can be resolved by putting new people into the team, but sometimes you just have to accept that it isn't a good fit and agree to go your separate ways.

So how do you go about finding the right PR support? Finding the right mix of skills and expertise, with the chemistry 'X' factor takes a bit of work, but it's worth it to find a good match for you and your business.

Five secrets for perfect partnership

Secret 1: Prepare the brief

Before you even start looking, you need to be clear exactly what it is you want to achieve. You can do this by putting together a briefing document, because you will save time and effort in the longer run by providing something tangible that the prospective PR team or expert can respond to. Often, a basic outline – maybe just one or two sides of A4 – will suffice for the start of the initial selection process, after which your chosen consultancy or freelancer can work with you to develop a fuller strategic PR plan if necessary. It may be that they will identify areas or an approach where PR activity may be appropriate that you have not yet considered.

Use the worksheet below as a guide and complete as much of it as you can. If you're not in a position to provide all of the information at this stage, you will be at least giving the consultancy an under-standing of your own expectations of the programme and the context within which their activity must operate.

Many PR consultancies struggle to get enough information from their clients, but, in order to be effective, they need to know as much about your business – both good and bad – as would any part of the senior management team. It can be uncomfortable to expose the soft underbelly of a business to outsiders by sharing this kind of information, but, in order for PR consultants to provide you with the right advice and support, it's vital to do so. Holding back embarrassing or confidential details just makes it harder for PR to solve some of the very issues that it must most urgently address.

Any PR consultancy should be happy to sign confidentiality or nondisclosure agreements upfront if this will help the process. If they are reluctant, then drop them from your list and go elsewhere. Trust is a number-one priority, so do what it takes to make you feel comfortable.

Here, then, is the worksheet to help you complete your PR brief.

Worksheet: The PR brief

About the business

1. Write a summary of your business and its key activities/products or service.

_____

_____

_____

2. What are your business goals? (twelve-month goals are fine, but include three- and five-year ones if you have them)

_____

_____

_____

3. What is your current market share/position in your industry?

_____

_____

_____

4. What is your current turnover and is the business in a position of growth or decline?

_____

_____

_____

5. In what markets do you operate and which will be expected to be included in the PR activity?

_____

_____

_____

6. How many employees do you have and how is the business structured?

_____

_____

_____

7. Who are the directors and/or shareholders?

_____

_____

_____

8. What is the major challenge facing your business today?

_____

_____

_____

9. Is there anything at present, or in your organisation's history, that
has had an adverse affect on its reputation? If so, how was it dealt
with?

_____

_____

_____

About the business environment

1. Who are your key competitors?

_____

_____

_____

2. Are there any significant market trends that are affecting or will
affect your business?

_____

_____

_____

3. Are there any barriers/red tape that may prevent you from achieving your business objectives?

_____

_____

_____

About your target audiences

1. Who are your target customers?

_____

_____

_____

2. Do you have any research/market intelligence about their habits/views/buying preferences?

_____

_____

_____

3. Who are your key trade audiences?

_____

_____

_____

4. How do you communicate with your employees at present?

_____

_____

_____

About your communications

1. What are the key trade publications that serve your industry?

_____

_____

_____

2. What, if any, PR activity have you undertaken to date?

_____

_____

_____

3. What marketing activity such as advertising, direct mail or market research are you undertaking?

_____

_____

_____

4. What sales material do you produce?

_____

_____

_____

5. How do you use the Internet and other aspects of IT to communicate (e.g.: website, email, extranet, intranet)?

_____

_____

_____

About PR

1. What do you want to achieve from PR activity?

_____

_____

_____

2. Have you set aside specific budget for this PR activity, and, if so, how much?

_____

_____

_____

3. How will you measure the success of the proposed PR activity?

---

4. Who in the business will be responsible for approving any proposed PR activity?

---

5. Are there people within your business who have received specific 'media training' or have experience of working with the media? If so, who are they?

Secret 2: Cast the net

Once you have written your brief, draw up an initial list of prospective PR consultancies and/or freelance consultants. Deciding whether to use a consultancy or freelancer will depend upon the amount and scale of work to be done and how large a budget you are able to allocate to it.

A consultancy will typically be more expensive, but will have greater resources in terms of both people and services such as in-house design-studio facilities and multimedia support. On the other hand, a freelancer offers more flexibility, often working from their clients' own offices and thus allowing greater integration and understanding to develop. After completing the worksheet 'The PR brief', you will be in a better position to understand what your needs are and, therefore, whether a consultancy or freelancer better suits your needs.

Get help with your search

In the UK, there are three main industry-backed services that provide assistance in the search for PR support.

PReview is a free PR consultancy-finder service run by the Public Relations Consultants' Association (PRCA). Go online, fill out the form and the PRCA will do the rest. Find them at www.martex/prca.org The service is funded by the member consultancies themselves, who, on winning a contract by this route, pay a percentage of their fee to the PRCA.

IPR Matchmaker Service locates suitable freelance consultants or PR consultancies from the membership database of the Institute of Public Relations (IPR) (www.ipr.org). There is a charge to client companies, who can choose to receive results by either fax or post.

Xchangeteam (www.xchangeteam.com) provides an all-in-one service for choosing a freelance PR consultant. It operates in a similar way to a traditional recruitment consultancy: Xchangeteam will shortlist, interview and recommend suitable candidates for your business. Fees are payable on appointment of the consultant, based on a percentage of their agreed contract.

As I write this, other services are due to be launched shortly, including a straightforward listing of all freelance consultants on the IPR website, which will give you a complete list of IPR members and their details so you can conduct the search process yourself.

In addition to these formal search services, don't forget to ask for personal recommendations from your own business contacts or companies who in your view have good PR. All the glossy brochures, website wizardry and slick sales pitches in the world can't replace the power of hearing someone whose opinion you value say, 'They're great – use them.'

Businesses in the US should contact the PRSA (Public Relations Society of America) for advice on local help available (www.prsa.org).

Secret 3: Make a shortlist
Finding the right PR support is rather like recruiting a new employee, and the same rules apply. Appointments made in haste are usually repented at leisure. Resist the urge to get it out of the way, and do this necessary ground work to ensure you find the right match for your business.

Once you have your preliminary list together, you are now ready to start filtering to reach a final shortlist (unless you have used a service such as the one Xchangeteam provide, in which case they will have done this for you). Make contact with all those on your preliminary list to ask for an initial credentials meeting so that you can review their experience, explain what you are looking to achieve (supported by your written brief document) and test out that all-important chemistry.

An initial conversation over the phone is an excellent way to make your first assessment of a company or freelancer. How was your call handled? If you had to leave a message, were you called back quickly? How helpful were they? First impressions, as they say, are very important and you can often get a good feel for an organisation by simply assessing how it deals with this initial unsolicited contact.

During the filtering process, you are aiming to arrive at a final shortlist of ideally three consultancies and/or freelancers. You will then ask them to present their proposals to you in a formal 'pitch'. Any more and you'll be in danger of information overload. Any fewer and you risk choosing by default.

Secret 4: The pitch

The pitch is where your shortlisted consultancies or freelancers get to present to you formally their response to the brief with a proposed campaign strategy and creative approach. Historically, this has been conducted at no cost to the potential client, but there is a growing trend towards the charging of a nominal fee by the companies who are taking part. In most cases, this is only a fraction of the actual amount that may be spent in both time and expenses in putting together the pitch, but it is an acknowledgment that considerable effort is involved. It also helps avoid the issue of 'idea rustling', whereby several consultancies are invited to pitch so that a business can glean some new ideas free of charge. Fortunately, few businesses are this unethical, and, by agreeing to pay a flat-rate pitch fee, you'll encourage an atmosphere of trust and professionalism from the outset.

Tips for perfect pitch

- If there will be more than one person involved from your business in the decision process, make sure all are present at each pitch.
- Give enough time for consultancies to properly research/prepare/present. Don't create undue time pressures to the detriment of the process.
- Allow enough time for questions at the end. Keep notes as you go and ask for clarification on anything you are not clear about.

- Make sure there is a discussion about budgets. Find out if the consultancy operates on a retainer (a monthly fee, usually on a twelve- or twenty-four-month contract) or a project-by-project basis. Absolute transparency is vital for both sides. No one likes surprises.

- Provide the necessary equipment as required: projector, flipchart, screen etc. Don't let the pitch be spoiled because of logistical problems.

- Agree a date by which you will respond – and stick to it.

Secret 5: Work together

Here are some do's and don'ts for working with a PR consultancy or freelance:

- **Do** respond quickly to your PR expert's requests, be they for sign-offs for press releases, for interviews or for pieces of vital information. A slow response can mean an opportunity lost. Remember that the PR consultant is working to the principle of the Three Golden Ws and meeting the media's needs, which means deadlines and rapid, efficient responses. Chris Davies of Grayling PR says, 'The most frustrating clients are the ones who hire you, then disappear. They are enthusiastic to get the programme going at the start, but then don't respond to your calls, forget to sign off press releases and delay approving activity that has been agreed to be part of the plan. It doesn't bode well for a productive and successful PR campaign.'

- **Do** allow a large enough budget to get the job done. PR costs vary tremendously, but many campaigns are hamstrung because of insufficient resources. The budget usually comprises (a) the fees that you'll be charged by the consultancy or freelancer for their time (much as you would pay an accountant for the time spent on your books); (b) the actual cost of implementing the creative ideas put forward in the campaign; and (c) the day-to-day running expenses that will be incurred in the execution of the campaign (such as telephone, fax, copying, postage and stationery).

- **Don't** leave your PR consultancy or freelancer out on a limb. Companies that bring together their various creative suppliers (PR consultancies, advertising agencies, graphic designers, multimedia consultants and sales promotion agencies) reap the benefits of the greater understanding that this communication achieves. It can also be very motivating for all the parties when everyone understands how they are working together to achieve a common goal. There's also the bonus of collective brainstorming opportunities and the avoidance of overlap, duplication and negative competitiveness that can exist among various suppliers if they are not part of a network of communication.

■ **Don't** be a bully. As the client, you will always have the last word, but remember that human beings tend to respond better to encouragement than criticism. PR people are generally not very thick-skinned and, as with most of us, tend to have a strong desire to be liked. This may be contrary to the stereotypical smooth operator so often portrayed in the media, but my experience over the years has revealed that PR practitioners don't do their best work for an overcritical client. Certainly, if things are not up to scratch, you have every right to complain and ultimately, of course, sack them if they still don't deliver, but it is not appropriate to lose your rag on a regular basis.

■ **Do** have realistic expectations. It is possible to get an instant result with PR, but it is more common that the programme will unfold over a period of time. This is especially true with trade publications. It can take up to three months before you will see anything in print, depending upon when the titles are published and when deadlines fall.

■ **Do** conduct regular and open progress reviews. Establish from the start how you would like to be kept informed of the activity and stick to an agreed schedule (PR consultancies will usually suggest monthly face-to-face meetings with more in-depth reviews on a quarterly basis). On a day-to-day basis, informal contact is now easily possible with email, but sometimes the telephone is more effective. Ambiguity can creep in when email is used, as it's not possible to 'hear' the tone of voice. If in doubt, pick up the phone.

■ **Do** say thanks. Certainly in the area of media relations, much of the PR work involves day-in-and-day-out persistence, which, for whatever reason and through nobody's fault, may not achieve its ultimate goal (editorial coverage in a particular newspaper, for example). This is just part of the PR job, but it can be demoralising. Acknowledgment of the effort involved is always well received. It's a small point, but it can be incredibly motivational and encouraging to hear those words.

■ **Do** make the PR programme a priority. Its success is as reliant on your commitment to it as it is on the skills of the PR experts you are using to work on your behalf. The enemy of this, of course, is time, but, as the author Arnold Bennett says in his seminal book *How To Live on 24 Hours a Day,* 'We shall never have any more time. We have, and we have always had, all the time there is.' His point is that it's not that we lack time – we each have a fresh 24 hours to spend every day – but it's *how we choose to spend* that time. What are our priorities? In our increasingly frantic 24/7 world, we are all looking for 'more time', but actually what we need to be doing is adjusting the time we have so that we accomplish what we regard as truly important.

■ **Do** remember to listen. Advice given by PR advisers is often ignored by businesses because it is unpalatable or difficult to follow. However, it's also true that sometimes PR advisers themselves can fall into the trap of purely reacting to events instead of seeking to direct them. Richard Edelman, CEO of global PR consultancy Edelman, believes that the PR business bears some of the responsibility for the dotcom boom and bust that happened towards the end of 2000. 'Instead of standing firm and advising clients to offer substance, the PR industry played along with companies keen to put the "buzz before the beef",' explains Richard. 'We took orders and got caught up in the perfect storm. The vital counselling and strategic role of PR was, for the most part, lost.' Although the dotcom phenomenon is unlikely to be repeated again in a hurry, the same unfortunately cannot be said of the relegation of PR into simply a reactionary tool.

How to spot a PR bluffer

With 67 per cent of CEOs believing that PR will become more significant over the next five years (according to the *PR Week/* Countrywide Porter Novelli CEO Survey 2000), finding the right PR adviser for your business will become more important than ever before. To help guide you in your search, here's a list of five warning signs that identify a PR bluffer from the real thing:

Warning Sign 1: I can do that!

Overpromising on what can be delivered by the PR programme is unfortunately quite a common problem (and sometimes exacerbated by unrealistic client expectations!). If your PR adviser seems keen to make lots of promises of coverage, be suspicious – but also examine your own desire for quick results at the same time.

Warning Sign 2: How much?

Nobody likes budget surprises, so make sure you go through the financial details carefully with your consultancy or freelancer. All PR advisers should timesheet their work and be able to provide you with a breakdown of time spent on a project against budget and a detailed analysis of costs incurred. Accept no less.

Warning Sign 3: Devil in the detail

Big ideas are all very well, but a true PR professional will be as interested in the nuts and bolts of the campaign as in organising big events. Ask to see examples of how they report their day-to-day activity to clients and whether they have a recognised good practice standard such as the PRCA's management standard or equivalent.

Warning Sign 4: Nice but dim

Having an open disposition is part of the make-up of any effective communicator. But make sure there's real substance behind the smile. Long gone are the days when all you needed to call yourself a PR person was a friendly attitude and the ability to lunch as if it were an Olympic sport. In an age when reputations can be wrecked by a careless remark or badly handled crisis, you need to be confident you've got the best brains on the job.

Warning Sign 5: Measuring up

No PR adviser worth their salt these days would enter a PR programme without having a good idea on how the campaign will be measured. If they haven't raised this with you, then you're dealing with someone who either doesn't know or doesn't care – either way, it's not good news for your business. A skilled PR adviser will work alongside you to choose the appropriate method of evaluation for the type of PR activity that you are undertaking.

When is PR not PR?

What is and isn't PR can get pretty confusing when the term 'public-relations consultant' is misused. For example, Max Clifford, described as a PR man by many, is a well-known figure in the British press because of his high-profile celebrity client list and reputation for brokering publicity deals between those in the public eye and the media. He has built a very successful business on negotiating with newspapers to sell his clients' stories. This is fine – but it's not PR in my book. I would describe this aspect of his work as more that of an agent. A PR person does not sell stories for cash. He or she will work at 'selling ideas' to journalists, i.e. seeking to persuade them to run a particular story because of its inherent news interest alone, and no money changes hands.

Agency versus consultancy

PR companies are referred to as either 'agencies' or 'consultancies'. Some may say that the language doesn't really matter, but I use the term 'consultancy' because that is exactly what the role entails being. The PR company's job is to advise you, to be a resource and to consult and guide you through the often difficult and delicate world of PR. It is unfortunately common for PR companies to be treated rather like lackeys – to do the bidding of their clients without having their views or advice listened to. It's like hiring a barrister in court, yet doing the advocacy yourself. A waste of money and expertise from everybody's point of view. A PR consultancy should be there as a valuable and objective adviser, which is why it is so important to get the fit right so that you have the confidence and trust to let it help you make the best possible decisions.

Section Two: Planning and managing a PR campaign – how to steer the right PR course for your business

The beautiful game . . .

The planning and managing process of a PR campaign is rather like working out tactics for a football match. It's all about keeping possession of the ball. Working out what the key messages are that you need to communicate, then devising strategies to keep them in play while keeping an eye on how you can score the next big PR goal will turn you into a pro before you know it. Unless you have a particular gift for PR yourself and have lots of time at your disposal, it's advisable to employ the experts – either a PR consultancy or a freelancer, or you could recruit in-house – to play the game itself. Your role should actually be a fusion between club chairman and team manager. You need to be detached enough to keep your eye on the bigger vision, hands-on enough to know what's happening week by week (and in some cases day by day), accessible enough to provide guidance when it's called for, and accountable enough to sign off materials and activities so that deadlines can be met and opportunities maximised.

The secret of managing a PR campaign most effectively is, first, to understand as much about the process as you can, and, secondly, to achieve the right degree of personal involvement. Too much or too little can be equally disastrous. Understanding the process means also understanding how a PR team works together. Unlike other creative service businesses, such as advertising agencies and design consultancies – where the personnel tend to be divided into strategists, creatives and administrators – the PR team requires people with a blend of all three skills. This can mean it's more difficult for those unfamiliar with how PR works to understand the dynamics and responsibilities of a typical PR team.

Called an 'account team' if in a consultancy or a straightforward PR department if in house, it's best explained by another footballing analogy:

The team line-up

First there's the team manager (account director or head of communications, the one responsible for overall campaign direction and team management: strategy, tactics, direction and team morale). Then we get centre players and midfielders (account managers, executives, communications managers, the implementers of the campaign who are responsible for getting your campaign messages translated into activities: getting the ball in play and moving it into position). The strikers come next (account executives, press officers, those responsible for 'selling in' the stories and ideas to the media and your customers: scoring the goals).

When it comes to defence, some of the bigger consultancies and in-house departments have specialists to deal with crisis-management issues, but the majority simply train their account teams to handle these within the existing team. David Beckham scores goals but also has to defend on occasions – and so it is with PR. It's an important part of the job to be able to manage both positive and negative situations.

Emma Cantrill, director at GCI London, has found that explaining the PR process in footballing terms can really help understanding and so cement the relationship between consultancy and client even further.

'Because the PR industry itself is constantly evolving and not as clear-cut in its format as, say, its advertising agency stable mate,' she says, 'then an important part of our job is to make sure our clients are familiar with how a PR team actually works. We can then forge a closer understanding and increase performance at every level.'

PR planning – where to start (or getting the ball in play)

First, consider five basic questions. These form the essential framework around which all of your PR activity will be built. They will prompt you to work out what you want to say, why you want to say it and to whom, how you're going to do it, and whether what you did worked.

- Q1: Where are we now?
- Q2: Where do we want to be?
- Q3: Whom do we want to reach?
- Q4: How do we get there?
- Q5: How did we do?

You will have already provided the basic information for Questions 1, 2 and 3 in your PR briefing document; but, if you have the funds, further research will provide greater clarity and focus. Your PR consultancy or freelancer may well include a research element as part of their campaign proposals. Question 5 refers to evaluation, which needs to be considered and set up from the outset. We'll be discussing how you go about this in greater detail in Step Five.

Question 4 is all about how to get where you want to be. This is the strategy bit (i.e. the overall approach) and is the cement that binds together the tactical bricks (the actual activities) of the PR campaign. The campaign strategy may revolve around one central idea, such as Monster.com's sponsorship of Job Shadow Day, which gave the Internet recruitment agency its key hook on which to hang related activities; or a series of events such as those the Eyecare Information Service (EIS) put together to promote good eye health in the UK over a long period of time, including tips for different seasons (summer holidays, Christmas parties etc.), pinhole cards for viewing the 1999 total solar eclipse and a series of celebrations for the annual National Eye Week event. Individual activity plans (tactics) were then implemented to gain maximum awareness for each event.

Strategy secrets – seven tips for getting it right

Tip 1: Think about context

Are you already undertaking other types of marketing/communications activity such as sponsorship or participating in a trade event? If so, consider how PR can support this activity and how much of the PR budget should be allocated to maximising this existing commitment.

Tip 2: Consider the focus

It's possible to have a successful campaign made up of individual activities, but look for a link (as in the previous paragraph) or main theme that can be developed for the whole campaign. It will give clarity and focus to the PR effort. A scattergun approach can work, but a rifle shot may pack more of a punch.

Tip 3: Be realistic about resources

PR is arguably more cost-effective than any other kind of marketing, but it still costs. It's no good firing on all cylinders at the start of the campaign only to have to cut back after six months because you've blown the budget. If you're using a PR consultancy or freelancer, remember that their fee is only part of the cost. To be effective, you'll need to allow budget for implementation too.

Tip 4: Keep it flexible

Have a clear vision about what it is you want to achieve, but keep an open mind about how you get there. Strategies that keep an element of flexibility in them mean the PR campaign can respond to opportunities as they arise. PR has a habit of producing the unexpected.

When the PR consultancy Julia Wherrell Associates booked the local MP to open a client's new operations facility near Huntingdon, it was just another run-of-the-mill business story for the regional press. However, in the period between the original booking and the actual event, the MP's fortunes were to take an unexpected turn. First, he became Chancellor of the Exchequer, and then, by the time the opening took place, it was the British Prime Minster, John Major, who ended up undertaking the facility opening as his first constituency event as premier.

'We had to do some radical amendments to our strategy to accommodate the fact that our little local story had now become a major news event, including the drastic ramping up staff and security, of course,'

Wherrell explains. 'The national media scrum was quite incredible with nearly fifty journalists and broadcasters turning up. It turned from an ordinary everyday story, to a really extraordinary event.'

Tip 5: Focus on target audiences
Strategies that try to be all things to all people are rarely effective. Keep your key audiences in mind and make everything you do relevant to them.

Tip 6: Use research
There are enough intangibles in the PR game as it is without adding guesswork to the picture. Increase your odds of success by arming yourself with as much information as possible and avoid the five P's (Poor Preparation Promises Pathetic Performance!).

Tip 7: Think timing
Your strategy needs a beginning, a middle and an end. While keeping PR central to your business thinking is a constant requirement, specific PR campaign initiatives will need to have progress markers linked to objectives so that you can constantly keep tabs on how things are going.

Talking tactics
When it comes to PR tactics, there are some tried and tested techniques that form the backbone of many PR campaigns. The tactical part of a campaign is where the real creativity of PR is unleashed as companies adapt these techniques to communicate their own particular messages. Here's a list of some of the most common techniques used in the tactical part of a PR campaign.

PR tactics

- award schemes
- editorial competitions
- exhibitions
- joint promotions
- sponsored booklets
- celebrity-linked activities and endorsements
- attitude/behaviour surveys
- sponsorship programmes
- journalist visits/trips
- charity-linked ideas

This list is by no means exhaustive and the challenge of PR is often to come up with activities that have not been done before or that have a completely new twist. A popular technique in recent years has been to use the power of celebrity in conjunction with a charity that is currently receiving media attention, such as Avon Cosmetics' Breakthrough Breast Cancer campaign (which had celebrities modelling special T-shirts for charity). Although combining celebrity and a good cause in this way is now commonplace, PR campaigns that feature this technique still can achieve outstanding results if timing, idea and 'message' fit are right.

It's sometimes easy to get carried away, however, by interesting or innovative tactics, but it's important always to link them back to the overall strategy.

Case Study

Cole & Mason is the UK's leading manufacturer of salt and pepper mills. In 1998, the business embarked on a consumer- and trade-focused PR campaign in support of corporate strategy, which was to concentrate all activities upon its core product range.

The PR strategy chosen was to focus on a celebrity-chef endorsement of the brand and its products. This approach had several benefits. First, British television was obsessed with cooking-related programmes at the time. You couldn't switch on a channel without being confronted by the latest celebrity chef dishing up his or her style of cooking. Linking Cole & Mason salt and pepper mills to a new up-and-coming chef ensured they were tapping into the trend of the moment.

Secondly, by choosing a chef who hadn't yet hit the big time but had all the signs he may just do that in the future, Cole & Mason could negotiate a deal that was affordable to them and provide the chef with a quality product endorsement that was directly linked to his profession, earned him additional fees and would gain him additional exposure across the consumer media – good news for his own personal profile.

Finally, in choosing a central theme for the campaign, it was possible to build up a programme of activities that revolved around it. The celebrity-chef endorsement was the cement that held the tactical bricks together. These tactical 'bricks' were a range of activities that took place over a two-year period, which included photography of the chef using the salt and pepper mills for distribution to the target women's-interest magazine media, a series of recipe cards featuring the chef's own special pepper-themed recipes – which were distributed at trade events and consumer shows – chef-hosted lunches for targeted journalists, cooking demonstrations at exhibitions, consumer magazine 'reader offers' that gave individuals the chance to attend a special cooking masterclass with the chef, and a series of postcards, themed to individual product lines and featuring the chef's photo and quotes about the benefits of choosing Cole & Mason mills.

Step Four summary

- Chemistry is as important as credentials when it comes to finding the right PR help for your business. Don't forget to include it on your list of 'must haves'.

- Being clear about what you want to achieve from PR will save you time, money and disappointment. Be candid about your circumstances so your advisers see the whole picture. Then they will be better able to help you get where you want to be.

- View the PR campaign as a team effort and remember to get involved, but not embroiled, in the action.

Step Five – Measuring for Success

Earlier chapters have mentioned the importance of measuring the PR activity you undertake. If, however, you're still not yet convinced that it's possible to do much more than measure the height of your editorial cuttings pile, I can't say that I blame you for being sceptical – you're in good company. Only a few years ago, a survey of in-house and consultancy PR professionals in the UK revealed that one in five did not believe the success of their efforts could be evaluated (*PR Week*/Countrywide Porter Novelli sponsored 'Proof' Survey/1999 by Westcombe Business Research under the direction of CARMA International).

With this lack of confidence shown by some in the PR industry itself, it's not surprising that those outside remain unconvinced. However, something of an evaluation revolution happened in the last few years, and the PR business has finally begun to get its act together on the issue. Recognising the pressing need for the creation of industry standards for planning and evaluation, the Institute of Public Relations (IPR) and the Public Relations Consultants' Association (PRCA) launched an initiative in the UK to create a co-ordinated approach to setting benchmark standards. With support from the industry's trade publication, *PR Week*, a research and evaluation toolkit document targeting PR professionals was produced in 1999 (and revised in 2001), to provide practical assistance and support to those working to the new industry guidelines. In addition, the PRCA membership is restricted to those consultancies that adopt quality management standards, including those for planning and evaluation. There is now widespread acknowledgment in the PR industry that evaluation is a must. However, this is not necessarily the case for businesses who use PR. So today's debate is less about 'How can we evaluate?' but 'How can we communicate the importance of evaluation and the case for research?'

Let's look briefly at why evaluation and PR have struggled to get along with one another in the past. Firstly, the PR business itself has been guilty of making do with evaluation methods designed for other marketing-related disciplines such as advertising and sales, and they have turned out to be pretty unsatisfactory. It's not surprising then that ways of evaluating PR didn't seem to deliver quite what was expected. Enthusiastic marketing directors who believed in PR, but insisted on judging the results of their PR activities in the way they calculated the value of their advertising campaigns ('advertising value equivalents' – see box below), were simply missing the point that true editorial coverage achieved by PR cannot be bought.

Secondly, the reason why PR evaluation was such a tough nut to crack is that there is no one-size-fits-all way to do it – no panacea that will solve the problem of evaluation in a single easy hit. PR is a complex, multifaceted, ever-changing beast, so it's not surprising that it's going to take more than one approach to get a firm grip on it. The principles of good PR don't change, but the techniques needed to measure it do, as it has evolved into a vital tool in modern-day management.

To AVE or to AVE not . . .

The AVE (Advertising Value Equivalent) method of measuring the worth of PR simply compares the amount of editorial space gained through a media-relations campaign with the amount it would have cost to buy that same space as advertising. It's a deeply flawed system: firstly, because advertising and PR are fundamentally different forms of communication; and, secondly, because the editorial coverage actually carries far more value simply because it cannot be bought. PR coverage is the result of a journalist's decision to run with the story, providing an independent viewpoint. It therefore packs a far harder punch than advertising ever could. In addition, AVE restricts PR evaluation to just the amount of media coverage achieved and not whether it has actually influenced attitudes, opinions or behaviour – the *raison d'être* of all PR activity.

The golden rule with PR evaluation is that you first need to know where you are starting from. This may seem a pretty obvious point, but many, many businesses simply do not know for sure and therefore struggle to get a true measure of the success of their PR. A business needs to establish right from the outset what its position is – with customers, clients, employees, buyers, investors, journalists or whichever group the PR campaign is being designed to address.

We'll be discussing how a business should tackle this shortly, but first let's look at the issue of monitoring PR success by editorial coverage alone.

If PR is about influencing attitudes, perceptions and behaviour, then the traditional measurement by quantity of cuttings or number of sales calls received is too simplistic to give an accurate picture of what is really going on. This doesn't suggest that achieving lots of media coverage doesn't indicate a successful PR result, but sometimes, if the editorial response is low for a particular campaign, this doesn't necessarily mean it hasn't worked on some level. Take the issue of whether PR affects sales, for example. PR will not always directly affect sales following a positive editorial piece, but it may well have had an effect on attitudes towards a company. Target groups such as consumers, trade buyers, key opinion formers (such as journalists and industry bodies) and city analysts may read or see or hear the information and begin to re-evaluate their opinion. So immediate direct action (as in calling a telephone number or logging on to a website) may not result, but ultimately, owing to gradual changes in attitudes and behaviour by the target audiences, increased sales, price points or enhanced brand value will materialise in the longer term.

Being bowled over by sheer numbers of press cuttings can also present a misleading picture. For example, one international fashion brand found that some of its European offices would regularly send in telephone-book-size cuttings reports while others struggled to make the minimum parcel-rate weight. On closer examination, however, it was clear that bigger wasn't necessarily better, as the smaller reports contained more cuttings of quality and substance, which more than equalled the others. Cultural differences were at work here, but, even if you don't have many different markets to worry about, do take a second look at what you're being presented with.

So what are the measurement options available to you? How do you know which is the most appropriate method for your particular PR activity? And how much is it all going to cost?

▇ A game of two halves . . .

There are two main groups or areas that need evaluation. The first (Group 1) is the media, or the channel through which you are communicating; the second (Group 2) is the actual target audiences you are trying to reach – the destination of your key messages. Remember that journalists themselves are usually a target audience in their own right. For example, if you are seeking to influence City opinion on a particular share-related issue, views of leading financial journalists are key; or maybe you want to persuade technology writers that your new invention or technical development is the next Big Thing. This just means that journalists are then included in the evaluation methods you choose for Group 2.

There are various techniques and methods used to address each group, which can be tailored to suit your particular circumstances. The methods are sometimes given different names, which can make it confusing, but essentially they are defined as follows.

Group 1: Media tracking analysis

Are we getting our message out?
Message delivery. This relates directly to editorial coverage and is linked to the key messages you agreed at the start of the campaign. Each piece of editorial is analysed against a content wish list. For example, a photograph of your product, a telephone hotline number or website address for enquiries, a quote from the management, a reference to your company's position in the market, and statements that embody your key messages may all be things that you would like to appear. Points are awarded for each mention achieved and then the total plotted out on a graph to demonstrate the frequency of these mentions. Alternatively, you could track each piece of editorial against a series of messages that are being broadcast by your PR activity (see Figure 1 overleaf).

Publication relevance and position. Content is cross-referenced against the importance of the publication in which the piece has

Message Delivery

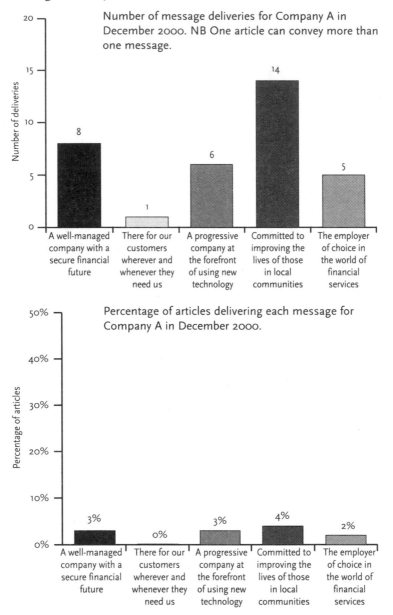

Figure 1 Example of how Financial Services Company A tracks the success of its Message Delivery across editorial in media (Source: Metrica – www.metrica.net)

appeared, its position in the publication and on the page. It's no good getting a piece packed full of all your vital messages if it's on page 35 of the *Grimsby Telegraph* and your primary target audience reads the business section of the *Sunday Times*. Context is all.

Audience Analysis

This is the method of calculating just how many people have been exposed to coverage. It is a fairly complex business and, to make matters worse, there are several approaches in use. Essentially, however, there are four elements (primarily used for printed media) that can be used to reach a result:

Circulation. The number of copies sold (in the UK, an independent audit by the ABC bureau is the official industry standard) of a publication.

Readership. This is the multiplication of the circulation figure by the number of readers per single copy. The industry standard is to multiply the circulation by between 2.5 and 3 times – for each copy sold, it is estimated that up to three people will read it.

Opportunities to see. OTS is calculated by adding up the readership of each piece of coverage obtained. For example, the British tabloid, the *Sun*, has a *readership* of approximately ten million (three times its ABC audited *circulation* of just over three million). Therefore, one article in the *Sun* would generate an *OTS* figure of ten million. However, two articles in the *Sun* would generate a OTS figure of twenty million – though this is the same ten million people being reached twice during the same evaluation period. OTS figures are often used because they generate large, impressive numbers, but can be rather misleading.

Audience Reach and Frequency. This is a more sophisticated analysis (as undertaken by Metrica). It takes into account cross-reading, listening and viewing habits. This essentially means that two articles in the *Sun* would have an *audience reach* of ten million, rather than the figure of twenty million given by OTS. Audience Reach analysis also takes into account the fact that some readers of the *Sun* may also read *The Times* and watch the *Ten O'Clock News*. Rather than simply stacking the readership/viewing figures together (as with OTS), this gives a more realistic figure for the number of people actually reached.

A further layer of calculation is added by looking at the *frequency* with which an individual may be exposed to the same message. If two articles appear in the *Sun* on consecutive days, it would reach the same individual twice. See Figure 2 for an illustration of Audience Reach and Frequency analysis in practice.

Competitor tracking/benchmarking

Analysis of how much and what type of editorial coverage is being achieved by your competitors is essential if you are to understand what is going on around you and within what context your PR activity is operating (see Figures 3a, 3b and 4). Anxiety that your competitors are getting a larger share of the action than you are can often be dispelled when you take a closer look at where and how this is happening. It can also give you clues as to what you need to do to offer something different or interesting enough to grab the spotlight.

The five elements of media tracking analysis we have just examined also work with broadcast material, with each programme or news item matched against criteria such as: Was a company spokesperson used? If it was an interview, were there any key messages included? Were product shots or company branding present?

You will be able to monitor the level of 'noise' you are putting out by using media tracking analysis. It is the most basic way of measuring whether what you are communicating is in fact being relayed via the media to your target audiences.

But how do you know whether these messages are being understood or acted upon? Again, taking the principle that effective PR is about changing attitudes, perceptions and behaviour, you need to know whether what you are doing is in fact having any effect at all. 'Raising awareness' of one sort or another is one of the most common PR objectives in a campaign, but unless you know what the actual level of awareness is before you start how can you measure whether it's been affected by your PR activity?

If you are to understand whether what you are doing is having the desired effect upon those you wish to influence, you need to dig deeper. One of the most effective ways of doing this is to begin measurement *before* the PR activity begins to put a 'stake in the ground', and then get feedback on progress along the way, which is what Group 2 evaluation is all about.

Audience Reach and Frequency

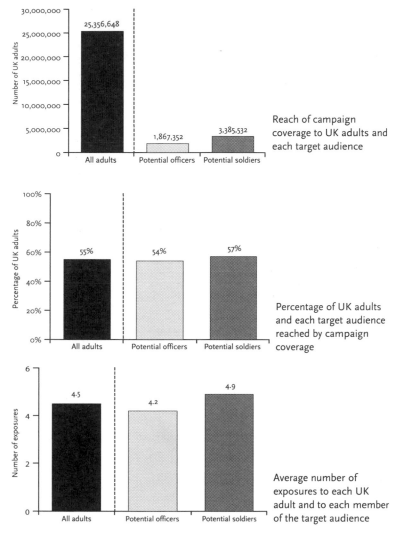

Reach of campaign coverage to UK adults and each target audience

Percentage of UK adults and each target audience reached by campaign coverage

Average number of exposures to each UK adult and to each member of the target audience

Figure 2 Financial Services Company A monitors the reach of its PR campaign in terms of two key target audiences
(Source: Metrica – www.metrica.net)

Overall Competitor Comparison

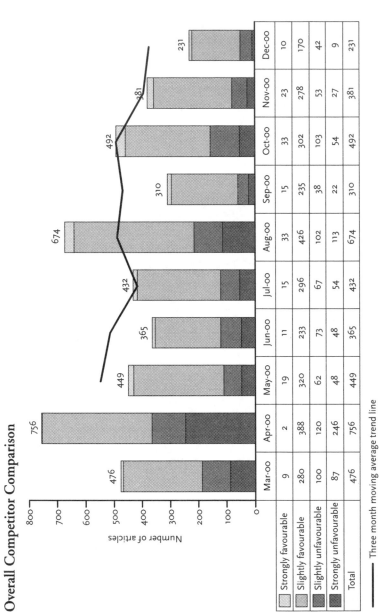

	Mar-00	Apr-00	May-00	Jun-00	Jul-00	Aug-00	Sep-00	Oct-00	Nov-00	Dec-00
Strongly favourable	9	2	19	11	15	33	15	33	23	10
Slightly favourable	280	388	320	233	296	426	235	302	278	170
Slightly unfavourable	100	120	62	73	67	102	38	103	53	42
Strongly unfavourable	87	246	48	48	54	113	22	54	27	9
Total	476	756	449	365	432	674	310	492	381	231

Number of articles

—— Three month moving average trend line

Figure 3a Volume and favourability of coverage generated in the national press for Company A shown over time.

Overall Competitor Comparison

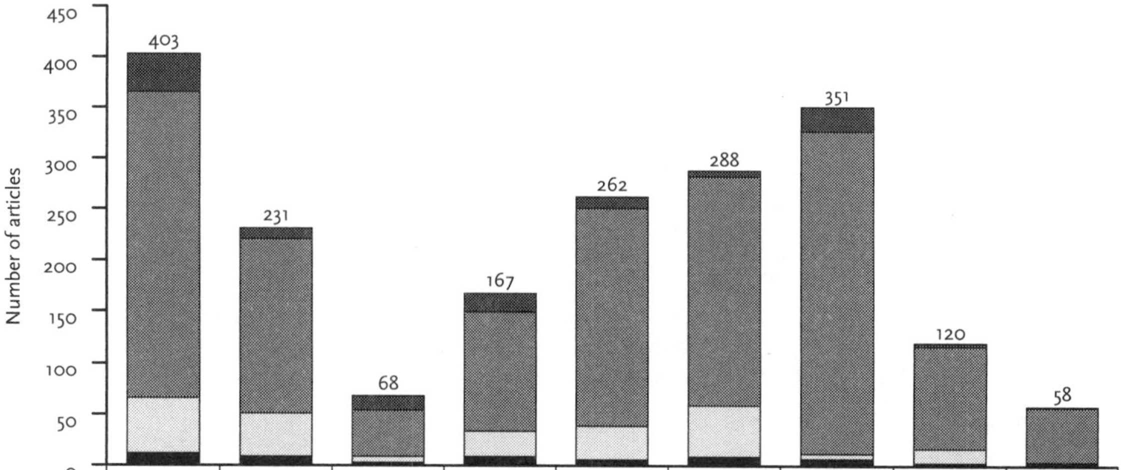

	Abbey National	Barclays	Egg	Halifax	HSBC	Lloyds TSB	Nationwide	Natwest	Woolwich
Strongly favourable	37	10	14	18	11	6	24	3	1
Slightly favourable	300	170	45	115	212	223	315	100	53
Slightly unfavourable	54	42	6	25	33	50	5	14	1
Strongly unfavourable	12	9	3	9	6	9	7	3	3
Total	403	231	68	167	262	288	351	120	58

Figure 3b A competitor comparison of the volume and favourability of coverage generated in the national press in December 2000.

Overall Competitor Comparison

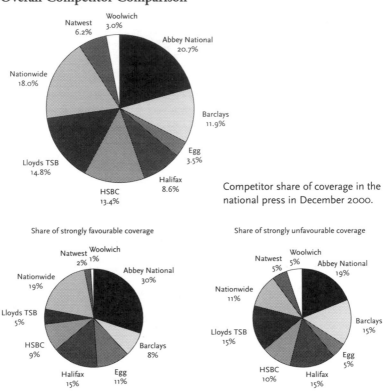

Competitor share of coverage in the national press in December 2000.

Competitor 'share of shout' of strongly favourable and unfavourable coverage in the national press in December 2000.

Figure 4   Financial Services Company A compares the volume and favourability of its editorial coverage over a one-month period with that of its competitors (Source: Metrica – www.metrica.net)

Group 2: Target audience monitoring

Are we being understood?

There are broadly two types of technique for monitoring your target audience: quantitative (quant.) and qualitative (qual.). Quant. asks the same set of questions to a wide base of respondents to provide statistically viable information (quant. surveys are also a popular media-relations tool used by PR experts to track attitudes and behaviour of specific consumer groups in order to promote everything from coffee brands to home insurance). On the other hand, qual. research provides in-depth analysis of people's attitudes and behaviour patterns – it puts the flesh on the bones of quant. data. There are many different formats and ways to conduct quantitative and qualitative research for monitoring public-relations programmes – here's a summary of the main types:

Surveys and opinion polls (quant. research)

Attitude surveys enable a baseline to be set to allow benchmarking at the outset of a campaign. Then they are usually repeated during and at the end to track any changes that have taken place. These types of survey can be bought off the shelf or tailored to suit specific needs. They are conducted in a variety of ways, such as over the telephone, face to face and by email, and are popular with larger businesses as part of their internal PR programmes. For example, levels of awareness and understanding of company values and activities are gauged to ascertain to what extent employees are positive brand ambassadors.

Omnibus surveys are statistically robust, wide-ranging surveys conducted by survey specialist companies to track general public opinion across a range of topics. Businesses can add a limited number of their own questions to omnibus surveys to address specific issues they are interested in. This is a lower-cost alternative to tailored surveys, but still just head counting.

Opinion polls are perhaps best known for their use in the build-up to political elections by parties and media alike to track voting intentions. Opinion polls generally work on a simple single-question basis and can be conducted face to face in the street, over the telephone, by email or fax. (For example, the royal household may wish to gauge the personal popularity of Camilla Parker-Bowles by asking the same question of the public each year – such as 'Will Camilla be Queen'? – and monitor the percentage shift of thumbs-up/thumbs-down each time.) Businesses can use opinion polls to question target audiences on a specific issue (e.g., a travel company might poll over-fifties for the most popular holiday destination or journalists might be polled by multimedia specialists on their use of company websites for gaining information).

Nongovernmental organisations (NGOs) or charities may use opinion polls to gauge the strength of feeling about a particular subject (e.g., 'Do you support the ban on hunting whales?') and then use this data to support their arguments/PR campaigns.

Panels and focus groups: (qual. research)

Panels are part of a type of survey in which a group of people are interviewed on different occasions over a set period of time about the same topics/issues. They are useful for a more in-depth examination of people's attitudes. For example, a manufacturer of leather goods may draw focus-group personnel from its local area to gain regular, informal target-customer feedback as new product lines are developed.

Focus groups are an informal discussion group, run by a moderator to a preplanned structure. They are usually made up of seven or eight people who are asked for direct feedback on a specific topic, issue, product or idea. They have been brought to the wider public's attention through their popularity within politics, although they have attracted some criticism for overzealous use by some!

Responses will be subjective, but can be useful for understanding possible acceptance by the target audience to your proposed activity, product or idea. Focus groups are used in many situations where in-depth information is required from a particular target audience. They are also used in the design and construction of attitude-survey questionnaires, where pertinent issues relevant to a target audience or group are identified.

Informal focus groups are useful to small businesses, who may not have the budget to conduct wider research but need to road-test an idea before taking it to market. When the Bath Archaeological Trust produced a series of leaflets aimed at the general public about archaeological topics of interest in and around their city, the draft leaflets were presented to a focus group for feedback. The trust wanted to ensure that the leaflets were pitched at the right level so that they were accessible, interesting and priced appropriately. Feedback from the group helped the trust make some valuable amendments before going ahead with production.

Quantitative (quant.) versus Qualitative (qual.)
The difference between these two research methods is illustrated by the results they produce, known as 'hard' and 'soft' data respectively. Quantitative produces 'hard' data (numbers) – it will tell you definitely how a group feels; whereas qualitative produces 'soft' data (words), explaining why they feel the way they do.

Are we influencing behaviour?

Ultimately, what every business needs to know is what, if any, effect its PR activity is having upon those it wishes to influence. The various methods of evaluation we have looked at here will help a business do this, but there are also a few other quick-fire ways to take the temperature of a campaign, such as:

- Website hits – monitor before and after a period of PR activity to track for increased traffic.

- Telephone hotline – calls can sometimes rocket immediately after a great piece of editorial appears. This is a good way to know instantly if your PR campaign is hitting the right media hot spots and reaching your target audience.

- Share price value – a good indicator of how the word on the street is going for a publicly quoted company. If your PR campaign is about keeping damaging stories and gossip to a minimum, the share price is one stark way to know if it's working.

How much will it cost?

Time, resources and money are the three obstacles usually thrown up by businesses when considering PR-oriented research. The IPR and PRCA recommend that a minimum of 10 per cent of the overall PR spend be dedicated to research. The ICCO (International Communications Consultancies Organisation) guidelines suggest a sliding scale, depending upon size of budgets.

My experience is that businesses often struggle to commit any budget to PR evaluation, mainly because to do it effectively costs too much for the smaller business. However, a way around the problem is to view research and evaluation not simply as a PR spend, but as a percentage of the overall marketing budget. After all, the increased knowledge and data will benefit the organisation as a whole, so why not take a broader view when it comes to allocating spend? By allocating funds to an overall market research budget (say 1 per cent of turnover), the burden is taken off the PR budget and spread more evenly throughout the business.

Counting the Cost

Providing ballpark costs for research tends to bring to mind pieces of string. However, for those new to research, here's a basic rule of thumb and where you can obtain more information:

Qualitative Research

According to the Association for Qualitative Research (AQR), current prices for a 90-minute group with a reasonably straightforward sample (for example, mainstream lager drinkers or mothers who buy cereal) and a summary report, range from £1,850 to £2,200; and a one-hour in-depth interview ranges from £500 to £650. As with all prices, these will soon go out of date and will vary according to whether you choose to work with a freelance researcher or a research company. For further information, go to the AQR website (www.aqr.org.uk) or call for a copy of the AQR 2002 Directory on tel: +44 (0)1480 407227.

Quantitative Research

Organisations such as Gallup, Mori and NOP all run Quant. research programmes such as Omnibus surveys. The price for an omnibus survey varies according to the type of question asked, but The Gallup Organisation, for example, suggests that one question to a sample of 1000 people will cost around £500. Looking at typical projects, a relatively straightforward set of questions for a press release will cost around £2,500 whilst a comprehensive series of questions (perhaps used to form a detailed report with associated press launch) will cost around £8,000 to £10,000. More information/guidance can be found from: www.mrs.org.uk/index.htm (see Useful Resources and Websites section at back of book for more useful website addresses).

Where do I start?

There are three routes that will help you kick off your research and evaluation activity.

1. Many PR consultancies undertake various levels of media-evaluation and research programmes directly on behalf of their clients, which is appropriate for many campaigns (some management and specialist-brand consultancies also provide employee and customer research services). They will also brief and manage specialist media-evaluation or market-research companies to undertake more in-depth and formal research programmes on your behalf.
2. Some larger businesses choose to employ specialist media-evaluation and market-research agencies directly. The types of service offered vary, but some agencies provide a one-stop-

shop solution, from media-impact monitoring to target-audience research programmes and in-depth analysis and reporting. Three trade bodies will help you in your search: (a) the Association of Media Evaluation Companies (www.amec.org.uk); (b) the British Market Research Association (www.bmra.org.uk/selectline); and (c) the Association of Qualitative Research (www.aqr.org.uk).

3. If, because of time or scale of the PR activity you are planning, you decide detailed tracking and research just isn't possible, you can of course undertake basic media-tracking analysis yourself. Time is the enemy of most, but even using the most basic method is better than none at all.

Worksheet: Research and evaluation: six points to ponder

1. Do you have existing research against which you could track your PR activity (e.g., data gathered for R&D, advertising or sales)? If so, what is it?

_____

_____

_____

2. If you are looking to raise awareness or increase understanding of a particular issue or product, be specific. What percentage change are you looking for? How will you be able to tell if this has happened?

_____

_____

_____

3. For message delivery monitoring, list five or six measurement criteria by which you will assess each piece of editorial coverage (e.g., photo, quote, mention of product brand, call-to-action number or address), or particular 'messages' that are key.

_____

_____

_____

4. Make a list of the media in which you are aiming to achieve editorial coverage and then rank them in order of importance (you can use this to give a 'publication relevance' weighting to your media tracking analysis).

_____

_____

_____

5. Consider the 10 per cent rule, but also think about allocating funds from elsewhere in the business. Don't let old-hat ideas about marketing spend keep vital funds that could be used for PR research fenced off.

_____

_____

_____

6. Finally, think about which of the evaluation methods from each of the two groups described above will best help you track your activity, given the budget you have available. If you are working with a PR consultancy, share the information above with them and get their input. Alternatively, speak to maybe two, or at the most three, specialist evaluation and market-research agencies to see what they recommend.

_____

_____

_____

Whatever method you decide to use, do make a commitment to do something and you'll say goodbye to PR guesswork for good.

Evaluation ground rules: six ways to get it right

1. **X marks the spot**. You won't know how far you've gone if you don't know where you started. Always establish your position before you begin any PR activity.
2. **Define success**. Take into account your PR objectives and set your success criteria accordingly for each area of activity. If you are a dotcom looking for investors, one appropriate editorial

piece in the *Financial Times* or *Investors Chronicle* may be all that you need your PR activity to deliver. If you are running a nonsmokers' campaign group, how many people are you wanting to make aware of the issues involved?

3. **Be specific.** As with setting sales targets, it's OK to be ambitious when seeking to raise awareness with PR, but you need to be specific about exactly by how much – 10 per cent? 35 per cent? 100 per cent? – and then match this against the budget and resources available.

4. **Resource it.** By all means beg, steal or borrow from other budgets if need be, but do put something in the research pot for PR. Few would undertake a £100,000 advertising campaign without including audience research. But that is exactly what many businesses still do with PR. Businesses happily spend in excess of this amount on PR and don't dedicate any funds to finding out whether the campaign had any impact. Crazy? You bet!

5. **Ask the experts.** PR consultancies should include recommendations for research and evaluation within their proposal documentation. Include a request for it in the brief just to make sure.

6. **Give it time.** Changing attitudes and behaviour takes time, so be sure to allow enough to let your campaign do its work. Remember to keep monitoring progress as it unfolds as well as evaluating at the end.

Step Five summary

- PR measurement isn't a luxury – it's a necessity if you want to find out if your campaign is working.
- Use research to track changes in attitudes, perceptions and behaviour at the beginning and end of a campaign.
- Break out of old budgeting habits and pool your resources to help find the funds for PR research and evaluation.

Step Six – DIY PR

DIY PR is a bit like DIY anything: it's OK as long as you know what you're doing and have at least some natural talent to call upon. If not, it's a bit like DIY shelving, or DIY dentistry: liable to go horribly and painfully wrong at any moment.

There's a mistaken belief that, when it comes to business, we should be able to turn our hand to most things, be it dashing off the VAT return or knocking up a quick newsletter on the PC. But everyone knows that you don't mess with the VAT man, and amateur newsletters look, well, just that – so the savings made by not getting in the professionals are often lost in the time it takes to put things right. In the long run, it's rarely cheaper, or wiser, to do it yourself.

Hiring professional PR advice is about tapping into years of experience – as well as specialist skills. You are buying into a wealth of knowledge that is gained through the ups and the downs of those who have been there, done that, many times over. And, even if you have the odd rookie or two on your PR consultancy's team, as long as they are supervised and good at the job it's no different from working with articled clerks or junior doctors. They will undoubtedly have endless enthusiasm to contribute – and at a lower hourly rate.

However, there will be those of you who, although convinced of the need to live and breathe PR in your business, simply can't afford to get in some specialist expertise at present. The good news is that, by simply absorbing the principles outlined in this book, you have ensured that your business has already begun to benefit from PR power. And there is still plenty you can achieve by understanding –

and experiencing – how PR actually works yourself. I don't advocate that you try to turn yourself into a media spokesperson or cutting-edge copywriter overnight – these are specialist skills that not every-one is suited to – but the more you know and understand about the process of public relations, the more you will get from it when you do find yourself in a position to bring in the professionals.

During the years I ran the consultancy, it was always the clients who had grasped the basic nature of PR who got the most from it – from its frustrating ethereal tendencies and constant ability to drive you to delight or despair at the drop of a hat, to the sometimes surprisingly humdrum path to getting a story used in the media. Seeking to understand before attempting to *be* understood isn't just some touchy-feely baloney: it increases your chances of results every time.

So where do I start?

A good place to begin is with these Five Golden Rules of DIY PR:

1. Set your goals and your yardstick
2. Establish the news
3. Be prepared
4. Have patience and persistence
5. Put PR on the board

1. Set your goals and your yardstick

First things first – a little bit of homework now will save you lots of time and money in the long run. Even though you're not going to be bringing in external help for the time being, complete the worksheet 'The PR brief' on Page 80. This will help you focus on what you want to achieve and get you thinking about what are the key issues you are looking to address with PR.

Then complete the worksheet, 'Research and evaluation: six points to ponder', which is on Page 113. This will help you consider how you're going to measure what you do. It doesn't have to be complex, but you do need to give some thought to how you are going to track your progress. Don't just leave it to 'gut feel'. We're all guilty of this sometimes, but, while gut feel can be a vital element in many business decisions, don't let it be the only rudder you steer with.

2. Establish the news

Most people, when talking about 'wanting some PR', mean they want to see positive editorial about their business, products or service in the media. Nowadays this can mean Internet media such as websites, e-zines (online newsletters and magazines), discussion groups, interactive newsletters, search engines and so on, as well as traditional print and broadcast media such as newspapers, magazines, periodicals, newsletters, satellite, cable and terrestrial television and radio. There are thousands of media outlets serving every interest, hobby or activity that you can think of – but they all (or 99 per cent – there's always the exception!) have one thing in common. They want news. There are varying degrees of news, and *where* you want to get your message heard (24-hour news channels want stories as they actually unfold; monthly magazines will go for general stories or themes because of the time delay of their publishing dates), will shape the *sort* of news you need to find and put forward for consideration.

Ask yourself the following questions in relation to the thing for which you want to get coverage (business, product, event, service etc.):

- What's different about it?
- What's new?
- What's changed?
- Where is it happening?
- Who's involved?
- Who should be interested and why?
- How will it benefit its users?

Now think about which type of media may be interested. Is it a story for your local newspaper? Maybe a consumer magazine will be interested. Perhaps it is something relevant to your trade press, or a specialist interest magazine. Is breakfast TV possible? What about your local radio station? Imagine who would be interested to read or hear about your story – what do they read, listen to or watch? Then take a look at Page 49 for some guidance on what makes news and see if your story fits.

Write down the main points of what you have to say. Use the tips on press releases on Page 53 for guidance and remember the Three

Golden Ws of media relations when getting in contact. More tips for working with the media are at the end of this chapter.

To illustrate how a business can identify its news and then choose the right PR approach, I've used a fictional example, Simply Angels, below:

Case study: Looking for an angel

The Situation: Jon and Angela Marsh set up Simply Angels, a service specialising in supplying personal support for busy businesspeople, such as collecting dry cleaning, waiting at home to receive a delivery, picking up prescriptions, doing the weekly food shop and so on. The company had already used PR to good effect by building a small but loyal customer base through word-of-mouth recommendation and then incorporated their good feedback into a lively website. However, new customer growth had now stalled and they needed to kick-start it back into action.

Budgets were tight, but they had taken some limited advertising in their local telephone directory and produced some good leaflets. They now wanted to use PR to help spread the word about Simply Angels by getting some positive editorial in the media. Using the worksheets 'PR brief' and 'Research and evaluation: six points to ponder', as recommended above, they defined their objectives as (1) to achieve three pieces of editorial coverage across targeted media; (2) to stimulate enquiries about their services; and (3) to increase the number of hits on their website.

By achieving these objectives, Jon and Angela would then have the opportunity of converting this increased interest in Simply Angels into new business. Measurement was to be defined by the number of editorial cuttings, message pick-up tracking, and hits to the website and calls to the office over a six-month period.

Establishing the News: Using the checklist questions opposite to consider what they had to tell the media, Simply Angels knew they were providing the first service of its kind in their area. No other business was providing this type of help for professional businesspeople. Jon and Angela were a husband-and-wife team who had previously held city jobs while bringing up a young family, so had first-hand experience of the pressures endured by many modern-day workers. Although their business was based at home, they lived in an affluent suburb of a large city, which had recently seen the arrival of two major international blue-chip corporations whose senior employees were ideal target customers for their services.

The approach: This is, first and foremost, a good story for regional newspapers and local radio, because it's a business serving local residents' needs. Jon and Angela could approach the business sections of their local newspapers to put forward ideas for a business profile. To give their information more appeal to the newspaper, they could offer to provide a list of hints and tips on how to manage domestic chores more efficiently.

The local BBC or independent radio station may be interested in the story for one of their magazine-style programmes. It's worth a call to the station to find out which shows accept guests for interview and then fax, email or call the programme researcher to put forward the idea.

This approach would suit the target audience profile on a geographical level, but, as their customers are generally middle- to high-income earners, they will also need to target other media. Therefore, Jon and Angela should also consider finding out about locally targeted lifestyle periodicals, which are delivered free of charge to properties over a certain value in some areas. Also, because their business taps into a topical theme often covered in the national media – the state of our cash-rich, time-poor society – Simply Angels may be able to get a mention in one of the lifestyle sections of the daily or national newspapers or women's-interest magazines. Another approach is to attempt to get their website mentioned in the numerous website round-ups that appear regularly in their regional press.

3. Be prepared

There's an interesting dichotomy in public relations. On one hand, you need to be able to respond to events as they happen, so you can use current events and trends making the news to your advantage (see 'Piggybacking' on Page 128). On the other hand, good preparation is one of the most vital elements in a successful public-relations campaign. Every PR expert knows it. Unfortunately, many businesses don't prepare – or simply don't appreciate the value of so doing. 'We want to PR the launch of our new sprocket,' they say. 'Great – when are you planning to launch it?' we ask. 'Next week,' they reply!

PR people are unfortunately all too used to this scenario. In fact, it tends to be the norm for many. It is of course always possible to do something in a short space of time. The current British obsession with complete home-and-garden makeovers at break-neck speed is testament to this instant-fix culture. However, in business, it's just madness to leave one of the most important elements in the introduction of your new precious idea, invention or service to the last minute.

PR not only has practical considerations such as magazine deadlines to consider (for example, monthly publications often work at least three months in advance and those Christmas specials you see in the December issues are usually put together in sunny August) but there are also all those potential opportunities that will be missed if you leave it all until the last minute. Joint promotions, competitions and teaser campaigns – not to mention tracking research and so on – will all fall by the wayside because there just won't be the time to pursue them.

So how do you avoid falling into this trap? Simply start thinking about how you can apply PR power right from the outset. Just doing the thinking ahead of time will mean you'll be open to ideas early on.

During the 1980s I worked in the computer entertainment industry as a junior press officer. What is now a multimillion dollar business was once a small, fledgling industry that was packed with many companies hoping to make it big. The process of software programming is notoriously slow and unpredictable, but, even so, those games publishers were masters at forward planning. PR was and still is considered a vital element because a game could live or die on the strength of a magazine review and the amount of exposure it received prior to launch.

Therefore, right from Day One, even before a new game had a proper title, it was already put into the PR schedule and timings, ideas and possible opportunities for promotion were considered. The game was still only as good as its programming, but by considering the PR options early – in some cases twelve months before its due release date – we were able to provide 'first glimpses' or behind-the-scenes programming stories and anecdotes as they unfolded. Consumer awareness and journalist interests were therefore engaged at strategic points during the whole run-up to the launch.

> *Every step you take ...*
> Sting's CD *All This Time* is a great illustration of good PR plan-ning. During the preparation for his special September 2001 open-air concert at his home in Tuscany, which was being recorded live for the album, behind-the-scenes video footage was taken, together with some interviews with Sting himself. All were put together with a couple of music videos of selected tracks from the forthcoming album and packaged in a joint promotion with AOL (America Online). This CD-ROM was then cover-mounted on to a British national Sunday newspaper and timed to reach audiences just prior to the music CD's launch in November. For this to work, someone was clearly already doing the PR thinking long before Sting even sang a note.

We don't all have internationally famous recording artists to work with, of course, but there's no reason why you can't apply this princi-ple of longer-term PR thinking to your own business. Maybe you have an interesting R&D (research-and-development) story to tell about your product or service. Or is there a personality or expert in your business who may make a good subject for a trade magazine's profile piece (this could be you!)?

Remember the media's interest in people stories, and see if you can ask satisfied customers to let you put together a case study of how your business is helping them. These can take a while to do because everyone needs to be happy with them, so start compiling good-news stories from the outset and you'll gradually have a library of ones to choose from.

4. Have patience and persistence

One of the most common frustrations with public relations is that results can sometimes seem awfully slow in coming. If we consider that PR is about ultimately influencing the attitudes, perceptions and behaviour of others, then it perhaps shouldn't be a surprise if this takes some time to achieve. However, it is human nature for us to want to see rewards for our efforts, or for something that we have paid for, and not many of us are that good at being patient. It's true, of course, that sometimes PR won't deliver the results you want. Not every campaign can be a success and not everybody can be persuaded to alter their behaviour or thinking to suit our purposes. But PR is the art of persuasion and therefore you need to stick at it.

In a review of the world's top fifty superbrands, the one common factor in all of these incredibly successful businesses wasn't good financial management, or even quality of product. Indeed, several had suffered difficult times and had to restructure their businesses completely as a result. The single common factor across these phenomenal performers was persistence – the determination not to give up, even in the face of sometimes overwhelming odds. We see this quality often in politics. Had the protagonists in the South African struggle for racial equality given in to the basic instinct for quick success, or become bowed by the sheer scale of the problem, apartheid would still be in force today.

When handling PR activity, give yourself a break and don't get downhearted if results are slow to appear. If you are trying to get some editorial coverage in a particular newspaper or magazine and it's just not happening, then take a step back and review the situation. First, consider whether you've got the basics right: for example, is your story really appropriate for the publication? Are you targeting the right section or person on the publication? What themes or topics are most likely to grab their attention? If you are satisfied you are doing all you can to meet their needs, then consider the issue of timing. It's rather like what happens when you are looking to win some new business and, by happy coincidence, you contact someone just as they are looking for the very thing you are offering: it's all about being in the right place at the right time. By taking a long-term view of your PR activity, you will be in a better position to get your timing right if you don't give up at the first, second or even third hurdle.

Patience and persistence – tips for sticking with it

- If you're trying to get editorial coverage, remember that media deadlines sometimes mean you won't see anything appear for a few months. This is particularly relevant to trade publications and lifestyle 'glossy' magazines. Many work on a two-to-four-month turnaround time.
- The PR business is all about influencing attitudes, perceptions and behaviour. We are creatures of habit and it can be a long haul to change.

■ PR doesn't operate in a vacuum. As with many other business activities, success or failure can depend upon other external factors. PR is particularly vulnerable to this when it deals with the media, as other bigger stories or world events may take over the agenda at a moment's notice and all previous stories get relegated or even binned completely.

■ If it drives you mad that your competitor has just got a huge piece about how fantastic they are, just remember that, as long as you are working at it, you'll also have your turn. Good PR is about having your fair share of the cake – not all of it.

■ Keep your PR objectives in mind and monitor your progress at regular intervals. If something's not working as it should, don't be afraid to revise your strategy and try something different, but remember to give it enough time. Undertake full reviews at the end of your financial year, when you should be in review and planning mode, anyway.

5. Put PR on the board

The last of the Five Golden Rules of DIY PR is to remember to keep PR close to the core of your business. If you run your own business, you'll already be an expert at keeping many balls in the air at once. That just goes with the territory. Experienced owner-managers or managing directors of small and medium-sized businesses often feel as if one plate is about to crash to the ground at any moment. If one does, and you are doing what many of the great entrepreneurs do – keep PR at the heart of their business thinking – you'll be better equipped to deal with the fallout that may occur.

While it may not always be appropriate or indeed relevant to be pushing for editorial coverage, as we've explored in earlier chapters, PR is so much more than just getting a pile of press cuttings. It's about communicating at all levels, with all stakeholders and target audiences, be they customers, suppliers, employees or competitors. By keeping your PR antenna switched on and taking a proactive stance on how your business is communicating with others at every level, you'll become less vulnerable and more effective.

DIY PR do's and don'ts

Do talk to your team. Good internal communication is as important as the external stuff. Just because you know what's going on, don't assume everyone else does. It always amazes me how poor businesses are at keeping their employees informed. There will always be some things that you'll need to keep confidential, but it's better to have both formal and informal networks for keeping everyone in the picture as much as possible. Gossip and rumour will happen anyway – so do as much as you can to keep the negative stuff to a minimum. And don't forget to listen to feedback.

■ **Don't** delegate. Every management book you've ever read may say that you've got to learn to delegate, and in most cases you should. But with PR there's some stuff that you should never let go of, such as being spokesperson in selected media interviews, especially if you're the one running the show. Clearly, if you have to do the PR yourself anyway, this is a great chance to find out where your forte lies, so use it as a learning curve. When you do bring in some additional expertise, areas such as strategic guidance, selected media interviews and participation in review sessions carry more impact when the boss is directly involved. By all means, offload the legwork, but don't dump the whole lot, or your PR effectiveness will certainly suffer.

■ **Do** expect the unexpected. One of the best arguments for making PR central to your business thinking is that, when a major problem occurs, negative publicity and poor communication can compound the issue, turning it into a crisis. Reputations are very fragile and all businesses are open to the risk of losing theirs. You can't always prevent bad situations happening, but, if you stick to the main principles of effective PR practice, your business will be in a position to deal with negative situations in an appropriate and responsible way.

■ **Don't** be afraid to call in the experts. Even if you are not ready to take on a full-time PR consultancy or freelancer, you may benefit from a PR audit that will assess your needs and provide a strategic plan than you can then put into action yourself. It is difficult for smaller businesses to justify the cost of the full consultancy works, but it is possible to get specialist guidance without having to take on the whole package.

■ Brainstorm your way to creativity

Brainstorming is a great way of stimulating creative thinking. Public relations thrives on creativity, so don't be afraid to arrange brainstorming sessions often, to help you come up with new ideas or ways to tackle communication issues. If you're running a one-man-band, the idea of brainstorming may seem a bit ridiculous: with whom are you supposed to brainstorm – the cat?

All is not lost, however: it's just time to call on some help from colleagues, peers and business associates with whom you feel comfortable discussing your business matters. It's often surprising how people from quite unrelated fields and industries to yours can come up with good ideas for your business. You can always offer to return the favour.

Five tips for brilliant brainstorming

1. **Size doesn't matter**. In theory, any size of group can brainstorm, but ideally groups of between four and six work well. With any fewer, individuals tend to feel more pressure to 'perform'. Any more and some won't contribute at all. But there are no hard and fast rules about this – just work with what you have available.

2. **Keep track**. The brainstorm facilitator should appoint a note keeper. Use a flipchart so that the ideas are there for everyone to see – it helps to see evidence of one's creativity! If the group is large, get two note takers so they can keep up.

3. **Have fun, but don't *make* fun**. The main objective of brainstorming is to stimulate creative thought – so the rule is that no ideas are 'bad', 'silly' or 'wrong'. Just make a note of everything. Filtering is for the next stage. The key thing is to keep ideas flowing, so no poking fun (a sure way to get people to clam up) and no analysing whether these ideas will work – just keep 'em coming.

4. **Use a warm-up routine**. It's important to break the ice and get everyone loosened up. A classic one I've used many times is the A-to-Z game. List all the letters of the alphabet on the flipchart and then go around the group asking everyone to contribute a word that begins with the next letter in sequence. Choose a topic related to the problem you're trying to crack (for example an A–Z of badminton if you are brainstorming ideas for launching a new racquet for the sport, or an A–Z of good service if you're looking for ideas to promote a restaurant). Keep it snappy and don't worry if you get stuck on a letter – just move on to the next. The point is to get the group talking and

thinking around the subject. This isn't an ideas-generating stage, simply the cerebral equivalent of warming up before physical exercise – you're cranking up the brain ready for creative action.

5. **Getting started**. Once you've done the warm-up, start by asking an open-ended question to get the ball rolling, such as 'How can we get our target audience to find out about our product?'; 'What can we do to demonstrate our product's effectiveness to the media?'; 'How can we attract visitors to our stand at the forthcoming exhibition?' Ideas can be collected as they are fired out, or collected at the end. Either way, there may be a lull at certain points, but don't worry. This provides you with the opportunity to run through what's been said to date and will give everyone a necessary breathing space before the next lot of ideas can come forward. If you've really come to a full stop, then it's best to adjourn and set up another session for the following day. Brainstorming often benefits from a break like this, when people have a chance to recharge their batteries. Book the session as early as possible before the clutter of the day begins. You can always bring in coffee and croissants and make it a breakfast brainstorm – the offer of food always goes down well!

DIY PR – targeting the media

Successful communicators know that working with the media can be rewarding, exciting and mutually very beneficial. They also know that it can be fraught with difficulty, frustration and misunderstanding. Many businesses fall into the triple-whammy trap of providing information that is either too much, irrelevant or too late, and succeed only in driving journalists up the wall. We've already talked about the Three Golden Ws in Step Three – the principle of getting what you want by working from the perspective of what the media need from you. Now we're going to take a closer look at some of the techniques and resources used when working with the media, together with some tips on how to avoid common pitfalls.

Ten tricks of the trade

Trick 1: Piggybacking

One of the classic ways of attracting media interest in your story is to ride on the back of some topic, subject or trend that is currently attracting media interest. By keeping a watch on what is hitting the headlines, what trends are being written about or emerging, and thinking of legitimate ways to link your own story to it, you'll increase the chances that it will get picked up.

In addition, wider issues such as health, lifestyle trends, family or work-related areas tend to be of evergreen interest for most newspapers and general-interest magazines. Many dedicate regular slots to these subjects with some going for full supplements, so if what it is you have to say links into any of these topics, targeting these sections is a good place to start.

Trick 2: Forward-features and events lists

If your target medium is trade or business-to-business, you can often find out what topics they plan to cover up to six and even in some cases twelve months in advance by obtaining a copy of their forward-features list. In the UK, several of the broadsheet newspapers also produce forward-features lists for their supplement sections, because these are planned and produced well ahead of the main daily newspaper. Some even have special fax-back facilities whereby you can dial a number and the list is automatically faxed to you. It's also possible to find out what events are due to take place all over the country.

In the UK, there are several forward-listing services, most of which now have online versions, too. The online service Foresight provides a comprehensive directory of events, launches, anniversaries, sporting events and so forth – and is an excellent tool for looking for piggybacking opportunities as well as a useful potential event-clash alert. Another such service is called Crimson, and provides TV broadcast programming information across terrestrial, satellite, digital and cable channels, with details of programmes either in production or on the schedule, so you can scout for any likely opportunities for your business to get involved. A list of useful websites is given at the back of this book.

Trick 3: Doing your homework

One of the golden rules of media relations is to know something about the newspaper, magazine, TV programme or Internet site that you are targeting. This means you need to know what topics are covered. Is there a news section, for instance? Are there regular 'people profile' pieces? Do they carry reviews? And you'll need to know the general layout or format. By understanding something of this, you will then be in a better position to know what will be of interest to those whose job it is to fill the space (the journalists).

For example, a home-furnishings magazine may run regular 'what's new' pages for items such as tables, chairs and lights that have just been launched, and have a slot for craftspeople to explain specific techniques used in building furniture. A business specialising in producing bespoke coffee tables, could then tailor their information – if it was appropriate – to appeal to these different sections of the magazine.

By taking the trouble to find out more about whom you are targeting, you'll not only be more confident in your approach, but will cut down on wasting time with inappropriate information and increase your chances of success. Simple, really.

Trick 4: Devil in the detail

If you've ever received a letter, fax or email that has your name misspelled, or contains an incorrect salutation or the name of someone who *used* to do your job, you'll know just how curiously irritating these mistakes can be. Most of us have been on the receiving end and probably unwittingly committed the offence ourselves – but, in the world of PR, being bothered to get someone's name right on a mailing list is one of the fundamentals of the job. Unfortunately, as journalists will testify, laziness in this area is all too common. If you consider your own reaction to badly spelled or incorrectly addressed mail, it should be obvious that, in order to give your information the very best chance of being read, it pays to get the basics right.

Journalists will also testify to the large number of press releases received that contain either spelling mistakes or grammatical errors – or both. It's a depressing fact, especially since many of these releases are issued by so-called PR experts. My view is that these releases deserve only one destination – and that's the bin. Everyone does make the occasional mistake of course, but try the following to help make them the exception, not the rule:

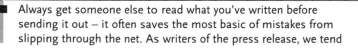

■ Always get someone else to read what you've written before sending it out – it often saves the most basic of mistakes from slipping through the net. As writers of the press release, we tend to see what we expect to see – not what's there. Even the most experienced of copywriters usually get someone else to check their words before they hit the 'send' key. My own best cock-up was printing an invitation for a magazine launch, which included reference to a new 'mazagine'. Horrible.

■ If you are building a database of media contacts, call each one beforehand to double-check that the information is correct. A brief call is all that's needed. You don't even need to speak to the person in question: the switchboard operator should be able to help. It may be a pain in the butt, but worth it to get a good, accurate list – just remember to keep it updated!

Trick 5: Creating your own hit list

One of the benefits of using a PR consultancy is that the majority will have access to the latest directories of journalists and media contacts, available via subscription from companies such as Medialink and PIMS. These companies provide online databases that are updated daily with the names, addresses, contact details and profile information of every publication and broadcast station in the UK (see Resources and Websites section for listings of both UK and USA suppliers).

However, you don't have to subscribe to be able to buy one-off lists from these sources. Checklists are tailored to your needs, with contact names, telephone numbers, email addresses, publication profiles and so on. You can also buy contact details in address-label format, ready simply to stick on the envelope. When you are starting to compile your target media, it is useful to begin with one of these lists (for example, our bespoke furniture maker could request lists with contact information of homes-and-interiors magazines, women's-interest magazines, furniture-manufacturing trade publications and national newspapers' Sunday supplement titles). It's likely that some titles won't be quite right (ask for the profile of each one, so you can find out what topics they cover), so you'll need to weed out the titles that are not suitable for your information. If you have time, it's still a good idea to call and double-check the contact details, as even these lists are not foolproof.

In the UK, it is also possible to buy hard-copy directories that list every known media organisation, publication and broadcast outlet in the UK. Two of the most popular are the PIMS UK directories and *Editors* – a series of A5-size books split into the various different media. The advantage of these is that they are kept to hand on the desk. The disadvantage is that, although produced monthly, they are not as up-to-date as their electronic counterparts.

Freelance journalists
Don't forget to include freelance journalists on your target media list. With a move by many media employers to reduce the number of full-time staff on their books, the demand for freelance work continues to grow. Some industries such as travel and telecommunications have a large proportion of free-lancers, who regularly get work published. Roger St Pierre, a veteran freelance travel-industry journalist and author, says that working with a freelancer means you often get more bangs for your buck. 'A freelance will fight hard to get material published because their own financial return is based on achieving publi-cation,' he explains. 'If his or her usual outlet doesn't run with the story, they will spread their net far and wide to see if anyone else will be interested.'

Trick 6. Handling cold calls

Dealing with cold calls from journalists can be pretty stressful if you're not sure of what you're doing. They can even be downright scary if the journalist is on the trail of a story you'd really rather not talk about. While the majority of calls may not fall into this category, it's always a good idea to be prepared.

Whatever the reason for the call, make sure you and your people are briefed on the best way to handle this initial contact. It will boost confidence internally and help ensure that any call from a friendly or otherwise journalist is dealt with in a calm and efficient manner.

Cold-call tips

- Give yourself time to think. If a call comes in, don't feel under pressure to talk straightaway. Ask for basic information such as where the journalist is calling from (it's surprising how many people forget to check this!), what their role is (news reporter, environment correspondent, researcher) and what their telephone number is – so they can be called back.

- Next, find out what the story they are working on is about. This is crucial, as it will give you the context of why they want to speak to

> your organisation. Find out who else they will be talking to and
> how they plan to use the information you may give them.
>
> ■ Tell them that someone will call them back shortly – and make
> sure you stick to this – even if it's only to say we can't help on this
> occasion.

Steve Ellis of MediaAble agrees that nobody in an organisation should give impromptu interviews to journalists and that it's important to be helpful, firm and professional when faced with such a situation. 'Gain as much information as you can from the journalist before attempting any sort of response,' he says. 'Remember the golden rule of cold calls – gain the maximum, give out the minimum – and that, no matter what the journalist tells you, assume you are always on the record.' But he also stresses that your aim should always be to communicate positively. 'Avoid taking a defensive stance and remember that, by taking the time to respond appropriately to a journalist, you are simply communicating to your business's maximum benefit,' he adds.

Finally, remember that like you, journalists are just doing their job, so keep it courteous even in the face of some who will be very persistent. Channel all media enquiries through to your nominated company spokesperson and, when time and resources allow, do yourself a favour and book a media training session. You may never have cause to speak to a journalist, but by experiencing some first-hand scenarios businesses often get to work through communication issues that they never realised they had.

Trick 7: Know your Net

There's a lot of anxiety about PR on the Internet. Should you do it? How do you do it? Where do you start? In the UK, the PR industry is only just putting together a set of guidelines for best PR practice on the Net. It's such a new, ever-changing phenomenon that we're all just feeling our way as we go.

There are two key things to bear in mind. First, the Internet has been with us such a relatively short time that, even though there are now people with good experience of working with it, we're all really in the same boat. It's easy to think that everyone else knows more than you – but, given that this technology has been in widespread business use only in recent years, and it is constantly evolving, they probably don't!

Secondly, in PR terms there are two basic ways of working with the Net: (1) by using it as another media channel, and (2) by communicating directly with its users via chatrooms, newsgroups, email etc.

Many books have been dedicated to helping businesses get the most from the Internet (including a book in this series by Tim Cumming) – but, for PR activity, read on:

Essential principle 1

Like any other third-party vehicle – be it TV, newspapers, magazines or radio – the Internet is just another channel for your PR activity. It behaves and works in an entirely different way for sure, but it is fundamentally one more route to getting your messages across. Don't be fazed by it – just do a bit of desk research to find out whether there are specialist sites set up to cover news and views on your business's area of interest. For example, many national newspapers have Internet sites, and most online versions do operate an independent editorial policy, so it's worth adding them to your media hit list in addition to the traditional titles.

Essential principle 2

The Internet of course provides businesses with the opportunity of talking directly to target customers, with complete control over how, what and when you communicate and present material. This means you need to use appropriate language, style and approach, given that potentially billions of people can see your unadulterated information. Don't slip into advertising-speak, though. Remember that PR is at its most powerful when it seeks to inform, not puff up. Remember also that site visitors are more likely to believe what they read if there is objective, third-party endorsement. Consider how you could achieve this on your site.

Essential principle 3

The rise of suck sites – websites dedicated to corporate bashing – means that, just as your business can put up anything on the Internet, so can others about you. These are generally targeted at major brands and corporations, but the ordinary person on the street has a voice as never before, so any disgruntled ex-employee, customer or even competitor can have a go at your business via the Net if they want to.

This means that communications and how you cope with such

attacks need more top-level PR attention than ever before. In the age of reputation, truth is all. It's no good hiding under the duvet if you find yourself under Net attack. Roll up your sleeves and get involved. One large corporation even went as far as to buy out the suck site and then employ the former owner to run it as a consumer-feedback channel. The saying 'If you can't beat 'em, join 'em' never seemed more appropriate than in the world of Internet PR.

Essential principle 4

It is said that over 45 per cent of journalists in the UK now use a company's website to source information – be it press releases, product information or images such as logos and photographs. However, there is still widespread dissatisfaction with the accessibility of many of these sites. Online press facilities or 'virtual press offices' are a great way to provide information on a 24/7 basis – but only if they are up to date and easily navigable. If you're directing journalists to your site for information, get someone unconnected with your business to road-test it first for ease of use. There's not much point if it looks great, but takes forever to download the information.

Essential principle 5

It's easy for a business to look as if it had a personality disorder if it's not consistent with how it presents itself, so don't forget that this now includes the Internet too.

The Internet has speeded up the exchange of information and enabled businesses to communicate as never before, but it has also opened the floodgates to a whole new set of problems all of its own. Here are ten tips to keep you afloat:

1. Keep **emails** short and sweet. Try to send them only to journalists you know are OK with receiving information this way. Information overload is unfortunately the price we all pay for having this fantastic technology at our fingertips.
2. **Fancy graphics** may look great on your multi-gigabyte computer, but, for freelance journalists and others whose machines are not as fast, download times can cause great frustration. Talk to your website designer about options for keeping download times to a minimum.
3. **Search-engine** technology means that Internet surfers can pick and choose exactly the information they want out of

millions of pages on the World Wide Web. This means that your company may be listed with a whole host of others, so get your site logged on to as many search engines as possible.

4. **Ease of navigation** joins download times as another crucial factor in determining whether a visitor will stay and explore or just click off. Make it simple.

5. Keep it **up to date**. Nothing looks worse than a website that is showing a date long past, especially ones that have 'latest news' pages. If you don't think you'll have the time to maintain it, take the date off.

6. Watch out for **other websites** that may have an influence on your business. For example, it's a fair assumption that Ford and Firestone keep a close watch on each other's Internet activities, as Shell UK and Greenpeace probably do, too. What sites do you think could influence your business? Are there any that you should make a note of to visit on a regular basis? List any that come to mind and keep a note of their URLs (website addresses) so you can take a look for yourself.

7. **Photographic images** can be stored and downloaded on the Web. Consider providing a library of images from which journalists can select – with both high- and low-resolution options. Again, speak to your website designer for advice on how to do this.

8. Assume you're always **on the record**. We touched on this above when we were talking about cold calls. Same goes for email and Internet communication. Emails are also now accepted as evidence in a court of law.

9. **Use netiquette**. If you are an experienced user of the Internet, you'll know that it has its own particular rules for communicating. If you're not, then look at specialist Internet magazines, which often give guidance on this.

10. **People power**. As Caraline Brown, MD of the award-winning Internet PR specialists Midnight Communications, says, 'The Internet puts power into everyone's hands.' Which means it's as available for you to use as a tool as it is for everyone else.

Trick 8: The contacts book

We've all heard the saying, 'It's not *what* you know: it's *who* you know.' In the PR world, there is no doubt that having a good contacts book is a great asset. Working with people you know and trust is something we all like to do and, in PR, building relationships with journalists over a period of time is an important part of the job. It means that, when you call, they will be more receptive to what you have to say – or at least give you the opportunity to put forward your idea or story for consideration.

However, although contacts do make the job easier, they are not vital in achieving results. Having a good story is. Every great 'contact' had to start with that initial call, email, letter or fax – so be brave and jump in. Remember the Three Golden Ws we met in Step Three, and start off as you mean to go on, with appropriate, timely and easily accessible information. You'll have a contacts book of your own before you know it.

Trick 9: Insider intelligence

One way to make sure that the information you are sending out to the media is up to scratch is to get the media to do it for you. In the classic tradition of those Native Americans who were trackers in the Wild West or politicians today who are invited to sit on PLC boards because of their understanding of government, a little insider knowledge goes a long way. Many freelance and some in-house journalists work for PR consultancies and directly for businesses on a whole range of writing projects. Be it features or newsletters, press releases or website copy, working with a journalist means you are able to tap their expertise and specialist know-how, all in one go.

Three points to remember

- Using a journalist to write your information doesn't guarantee it will be used in the publications or programmes you are targeting. This is still a PR approach.

- Using a well-known journalist from your industry can add kudos to the material you are producing: for example, if they guest-edit your company newsletter or write a booklet or guide that is being sponsored by your business.

> ■ There may be issues of conflict of interest in some cases (usually when working with in-house journalists). You'll need to check with the journalist first whether the project you have in mind puts them at odds with their employers.

Trick 10: Don't be 'me too' – be 'me different'!

The media are always looking for an interesting, different or unusual angle, so, in order to attract their attention, you'll need to give them what they want. Even if what you have to say isn't particularly interesting, different or unusual, your approach to the media can be.

Case study: Sourceree

The situation: At the height of the dotcom boom, Sourceree, a start-up dotcom business specialising in the supply-chain event management (SCEM) industry faced two key challenges: first, to grow a client base from a select group of blue-chip companies and, secondly, to attract further venture-capital investment. They had little funds available for marketing, so decided to concentrate what they had on focused PR activity.

Working with a freelance business-to-business PR specialist, Annie Garthwaite, they identified two main PR goals. One was to achieve media coverage in target press, which would fuel potential client interest and attract the attention of potential venture capitalists (a target was set of five pieces in titles such as *Red Herring* magazine, the *FT, The Times* and the *Infoconomist*). The second was to increase awareness and build the all-important word-of-mouth reputation. (There was no empirical research available on current levels of awareness, so they would have to measure this on the feedback they received when approaching new business prospects.)

The strategy: The problem was that there were so many other start-ups fighting for media attention that only the really quirky ones, or those focused on a consumer rather than the business-to-business market, were grabbing the headlines.

'The client had a great product and a brilliant idea – but, because we were dealing in a fairly dry subject, we needed a twist to give our story its own kind of quirkiness,' Garthwaite explains. She therefore proposed a strategy that would turn the usual 'isn't our technology clever?' approach used by so many other dotcoms on its head. 'We decided to make a virtue out of being boring.'

So, instead of talking 'technology stacks' and 'group portals', they talked about their experience in the SCEM market and how 'old-economy' businesspeople were using the power of the internet to solve deep seated and age-old problems that had dogged the business world for years. Focusing on the reputations and experience of the company's directors, Garthwaite was able to set up several media interviews to discuss the wider issues facing the SCEM industry and, of course, how their product would help facilitate a new way forward. In addition, to support their argument, research was used to illustrate the scale of losses incurred by companies whose supply-chain management systems were inefficient.

The result: 'The campaign was a great success,' says Garthwaite. 'We not only received extensive editorial coverage in the right places, far exceeding our target of five pieces: the company was the only non-US business to be named in the leading business Internet magazine *Red Herring*'s prestigious "10 To Watch" listing for 2001 and *Infoconomist*'s top ten list of most promising start ups.' In fact, the company managed to achieve all of its objectives. Sales enquiries were received from the company's targeted group of potential customers who had read about it in the media, and vital first-round venture-capitalist funding secured.

Step Six summary

- DIY PR is not for everyone, it's too easy to hammer your own thumb.

- However, every business can benefit from understanding the basics, so don't worry too much if you are left holding the baby in the short term. The more you know about the PR process, the better your chances of success in the long run.

- DIY PR can be a sobering and ultimately very useful experience for when you are in a position to bring in the experts.

Campaign File – Examples from Seven Real Businesses

From giant corporations to medium-size businesses and individual entrepreneurs, the following seven case studies demonstrate how PR power is being harnessed by some in the business world today. Each case study illustrates a specific approach or way that PR has been used to help achieve corporate goals. I hope they will inspire you to use it to do the same!

1. Italian Secrets – *Spreading The Word*
2. Piaggio – *Art Vespa*
3. SDL – *Going Global*
4. McVitie's – *National Dunking Day*
5. The Lowry – *Opening Launch*
6. Bupa – *One Life*
7. Vodafone – *New HQ*

Campaign File 1: Small business generating national interest

Italian Secrets – Spreading The Word

'We use highly personalised targeting of a small number of key journalists to unleash the miracle of PR.' – **Anna Venturi, Founder, Italian Secrets Cookery School**

Business background and objectives:

Anna Venturi, founder of The Italian Secrets Cookery School in Beaconsfield, Buckinghamshire, combines her cookery school with a gourmet shop and catering service for the southeast area of England. The common theme in Anna's three ventures is the promotion of the very best of Italian cooking – using the finest ingredients – to a discerning and high income audience.

Six years ago the cookery school relocated from the kitchen of Anna's Buckinghamshire home to a purpose-built culinary arena with adjacent shop in Beaconsfield. At this point Italian Secrets became a serious business whose key objectives were to secure local, regional and national visitors for its day courses in Italian cookery, as well as national recognition for the associated shop. Italian Secrets planned to measure the success of the relocation via financial indicators such as profitability and rate of growth of sales.

PR objectives:

Italian Secrets uses PR as the mainstay of its marketing effort, combined with selected classified advertising and database mailings. Anna is a great believer in 'the miracle of PR' and has been using independent PR consultant Suzanne Howe for over four years. The main objectives of the PR campaign are to promote Italian Secrets to the readers of the national press and the top women's and home magazines, for example *BBC Good Food* and *Homes and Gardens*. The single most important objective of the PR activity is for Italian Secrets to be known as *the* Italian Cookery School in the UK by journalists and target public alike. This would be measured according to the quality and frequency of press coverage in the target media and by monitoring sales and enquiries which resulted from specific pieces of editorial.

Strategy:

By using the influence and authority of editorial, Suzanne carries out a highly targeted and very effective approach to PR, which aims to generate and sustain excellent media contacts and associated press coverage. To this end Suzanne identified twenty key journalists from the national and women's media and targeted them on a one-to-one basis. They are regularly contacted with press releases, recipes, feature ideas and samples from the gourmet shop and many have personally experienced the Italian Secrets cookery classes. The close relationships that have developed mean that many journalists now call Anna direct for recipes or ideas to supplement a feature they are writing.

In addition to the primary target of those 20 key media, there is a broader mailing list of 160 press contacts. They receive general mailings, for example launching the annual Italian Secrets calendar.

Results and evaluation:

In accordance with the original campaign goals, the progress of the PR campaign is monitored by the quality of press coverage from the key target media and the reader enquiries this coverage generates.

PR success also directly affects the bottom line by encouraging third party endorsement of the products by the media. For example, *BBC Good Food* magazine published a feature which included a number of Anna's recipes, which said 'buy nougat from Italian Secrets' and 200 people did! The success of the PR strategy is also assessed in other ways, for example by the frequency with which journalists proactively contact Italian Secrets for comment or input into feature articles. This shows that the company's profile is now well established with one of their most important audiences – the media themselves.

Suzanne comments: 'We believe the work undertaken to raise the profile of Italian Secrets has also created an even greater interest by the public and media in Italian food and Italian cookery. Italian Secrets has a good product to sell, which, coupled with the level of interest by the magazines, has meant that we are able to provide exactly what they want, which is why the PR campaign has been such a success.'

www.italiansecrets.co.uk

Campaign File 2 – Use of celebrity and charity association

PIAGGIO – Art Vespa

'Art Vespa had all the right ingredients: originality, wit, style, celebrity endorsement and a worthwhile cause. It enhanced the image of Vespa as a style icon and collectors' item.' – **Costantino Sambuy, Marketing Manager, Piaggio Ltd**

Business background and objectives:

As the first-ever scooter, invented in 1946, Vespa is a mature brand with a heritage of over fifty years. Manufacturer Piaggio needed to maintain a high consumer profile for Vespa, despite the fact that no new Vespa products had been launched for four years.

PR objectives:

As part of its ongoing consumer work for Piaggio and its three scooter brands – Piaggio, Vespa and Gilera – Focus PR was asked to organise an event to enhance Vespa's image as a style icon. The event would have to be strong enough to generate media coverage in the absence of a news angle or product launch. The key PR objectives were to secure widespread consumer media coverage, to increase visibility of the brand, particularly among the key target audience of 18–30 year olds and to reinforce the aspirational positioning of Vespa. This would be measured by a detailed evaluation of target media and support of the various events.

Strategy:

Focus PR chose to reinforce the iconic status and popularity of the Vespa in the UK by inviting British celebrities to design their dream Vespa. Eight celebrities from music, film, fashion and the arts (David Bailey, Donna Air, Helen Fielding, Simon le Bon, Nick Moran, Rhys Ifans, Steps and Jasper Conran) produced designs that were brought to life by a specialist customiser.

The scooters were then exhibited and auctioned at Sotheby's in aid of the charity Action on Addiction. The Vespa customised by Salvador Dali in 1962 was borrowed from the Guggenheim Museum in Bilbao, Spain, so that it could be exhibited at Sotheby's alongside the eight new designs. The scooters were on display for a week, during which time media interviews were carried out at Sotheby's and members of the public were able to view the lots. A champagne reception and the auction were held on the closing night of the exhibition, attended by celebrities, the media, bidders and guests.

To increase visibility of the project among Vespa's target audience, and to give it aspirational yet accessible appeal, a parallel competition invited the public to join the celebrities in designing their own dream Vespa. The prize was to have their design exhibited at Sotheby's and to have a Vespa ET2 customised to their specifications. The public competition ran through the *Guardian* and the *Independent*, Piaggio's website and 100,000 leaflets distributed nationwide via Top Shop and Top Man stores, plus arts and design venues. Vespa scooters were also placed in the windows of eight regional Top Shop flagship stores, including Oxford Circus in London. The winning design, the A to Z Vespa, was brought to life and Piaggio subsequently used it for promotional activity before presenting it to the winner.

The project provided numerous story angles for the media such as celebrity style features, 'the original scooter gets a new look', the must-have shopping item, and interviews with celebrity participants.

Results and evaluation:

The project received extensive print and broadcast coverage, nationally, regionally and internationally. Highlights of the print coverage include *The Times, Daily Telegraph, Evening Standard, Daily Express, Metro, OK!, Scotsman* and *BBC Top Gear* magazine.

In all, there were 67.2 million opportunities to see (based on print media readership, not including television and radio coverage); 11 national newspapers and consumer magazines; 29 regional/local newspapers; 6 specialist magazines; 7 TV programmes (5 in the UK and 2 in Italy); 1 radio programme (LBC radio) and 5 websites. Over 120 key messages were delivered.

The auction was attended by 200 people and raised nearly £20,000 for Action on Addiction. In addition, high visibility was achieved through the public competition – with over 400 entries received.

The Art Vespa PR campaign won 'Best Promotional Activity' in the *PR Week* Awards 2001 and Piaggio now uses the core concept on an annual basis.

www.focuspr.co.uk

www.piaggio.com

Campaign File 3 – Business to business

SDL INTERNATIONAL – Going Global

'The SDL International campaign ensured maximum exposure within all target media sectors.' – **Caraline Brown, CEO, Midnight Communications**

Business background and objectives:

Founded in 1992 and fully listed on the London Stock Exchange, SDL International is a leading provider of globalisation technologies and services. Its offerings, which enable companies to remove cultural and linguistic barriers to international trade, include multilingual content management, real-time translation technologies, translation memory and a full range of in-house consulting and localisation services.

Although established with headquarters in the UK, the UK media displayed a very low awareness of SDL International, particularly within the Technology and Business sectors.

PR objectives:

In 2000 Midnight Communications was appointed by SDL International to build the company's profile in line with the aim of being 'the UK's leading globalisation solutions provider'. Particular attention was given to its target trade publications including the computing, new media and business press. The success of the campaign would be evaluated according to the quality and quantity of press coverage in these media sectors.

Strategy:

The first task was to conduct a media audit to determine current industry awareness of SDL International and the broader issues of globalisation and localisation. Media awareness of SDL International was very low, with a mere 33 per cent of respondents recognising the company. Of these, only 6 per cent claimed to understand the company's business. Furthermore, the term 'globalisation' was generally associated with anti-Capitalist May Day riots – a far cry from translation and localisation!

Midnight therefore devised an issues-based campaign to bring life and meaning to the term 'globalisation', and to educate the market on the importance of effective multilingual communication. The campaign, which used a variety of PR tactics, would highlight the fact that translation is not enough – cultural adaptation is key.

SDL International and its CEO, Mark Lancaster, were positioned to the media as key commentators on global communication and content management strategies. Credibility was generated through informed comment and advice.

Research was conducted into the size of the translation market, the most popular languages on the Internet, and examples of companies that have successfully adapted a local approach to their web site content. Research also focused on cultural issues to be addressed when entering key overseas markets, amusing examples of multinationals' mistranslations and cultural faux pas, as well as analyst research into key emerging markets.

In addition to generating quality news stories, the research was used to develop a series of strategic articles. The articles highlighted the opportunities offered by a global approach, as well as practical advice on how to implement a global communications strategy from CEO Mark Lancaster. By-lined articles appeared in six target publications including: *Industry Standard, New Media Creative* and *Sales Director*. The media-relations campaign generated a further fourteen features addressing the issue of globalisation and translation.

A number of press trips and product demonstrations were also organised to introduce SDL International personnel to key media. Case studies of SDL clients who had implemented successful overseas strategies were produced and issued to target media. New client win and partner stories were used regularly to encourage further blue-chip partnerships. To give the story visual impact, creative photography of Mark Lancaster spinning a high-tech globe like a basketball on his finger, was developed.

To encourage strategic partnerships within the industry, Midnight orchestrated an SDL-branded round-table discussion forum to discuss the issues central to global content management. This event brought together high-profile players from companies such as Adobe, Accenture, Organic and Media Surface. The round-table enforced SDL's position as a leading innovator in the field of globalisation, and served to encourage further strategic partnerships.

Results and evaluation:

The ongoing PR campaign for the company generated trade, IT, new media and Internet results, with positive media coverage appearing in all key trade titles, resulting in over twelve million opportunities to see (OTS).

Language and translation have been successfully linked to globalisation within SDL International's target market, with the key message that 'it's not enough to translate – you have to consider local culture' being effectively communicated.

www.sdlintl.com

www.midnight.co.uk

■ Campaign File 4 – Use of research

McVitie's – National Dunking Day

'The reason the story worked so well was that McVitie's was inextricably linked to a genuinely newsworthy and entertaining piece of research, rather than relying on a stunt alone to generate the interest in National Dunking Day.' – **Tricia Beaumont, Director, Lexis PR**

Business background and objectives:

McVitie's had a mission to build its association with hot drinks. Research had identified that there was a huge opportunity to grow sales if the nation's tea and coffee drinkers could be encouraged to accompany more 'drink occasions' with a biscuit. The company created National Dunking Day in 1995 in response to this challenge, but media coverage had become limited to picture-led national and regional coverage and 'special interest day' snippets. The trade audience was under-whelmed with the concept and the interest it generated amongst consumers and the strategy behind a link for McVitie's and dunking had been lost. The challenge was to deliver a high profile, indelible link between the products and hot drinks.

PR objectives:

There were two objectives: to reinforce the McVitie's brand as the UK's leading 'authority on biscuits' and to highlight the link between McVitie's biscuits and hot drinks. The PR strategy developed by Lexis PR for the Dunking Day project was therefore to position McVitie's as the world's leading authority on dunking, and bring the famous British ritual up to date in the process. The success of this strategy would be evaluated according to the resulting media coverage, with a range of criteria such as the number of people reached, the volume of national press articles and the communication of key messages.

Strategy:

The requirement was for a news story that the country – and, as it turned out, the world – would want to hear about, which delivered against these criteria. Lexis' proposal was to commission a piece of serious academic research into the 'Science of Dunking' and discover an equation for the perfect dunk that could be 'owned' and exploited by McVitie's.

Lexis commissioned Dr Len Fisher, an independent honorary research fellow at Bristol University's physics department, to apply the principles of physics to the 'dunking capacity' of a range of McVitie's biscuits. The research would explain the reasons why and how people should dunk – as it turned out, proving that dunking releases more flavour than a non-dunked biscuit. The equation for dunking, together with *in situ* shots of the biscuits and the Bristol laboratory, provided the vital news and visual hooks.

Before the research project was completed, Lexis briefed BBC News Gathering exclusively and worked with a team to deliver pieces for Radio Four's *Today*, the *One O'Clock News*, BBC Online and BBC News 24. Journalists and film/radio crews were allowed behind-the-scenes access to Dr Fisher and his team while the experiments were underway.

The McVitie's Science of Dunking Report was launched at an early-morning media conference at the suitably scientific Novartis Foundation in London. The report was given to the *Evening Standard* for coverage the evening before the launch, to set the scene for the broadcast coverage the following day. *Today* radio news and feature pieces on the morning of the launch tweaked media interest, as did the feature on the BBC's website. Radio interviews – both ad hoc and set up in advance – were held throughout the day and filming for Channel Five was completed in time for its 7 p.m. news. International TV and radio interviews – by US, Australian and South African crews – carried on throughout the week.

Results and evaluation:

Lexis used CMS Precis to evaluate the UK media coverage. One hundred and thirty-four items were generated in ninety-seven different media (including every UK national daily apart from the *Independent*). The Precis report stresses the high number of branded mentions – 75 per cent – as well as the strong visual branding. The national press, which accounted for 10 per cent of the coverage by volume, had over 50 per cent of the 'coverage by impact' thanks to the in-depth reporting of the story. Two important key messages – that 'McVitie's biscuits are the best for dunking' and 'McVitie's biscuits are perfect with a hot drink' – accounted for 39 per cent and 27 per cent of the total message communication respectively.

Sales uplift around the time of Dunking Day cannot be credited to the PR campaign alone as there was significant retail promotion of the event, although no above-the-line advertising. The campaign won PR Week's 'Best Use of Research' award in 1999.

www.lexispr.com
www.unitedbiscuits.co.uk

Campaign File 5: Event PR

The Lowry – Opening Launch

'This single local media event lead to literally hundreds of press cuttings and thousands of enquiries from the public.' – **Michelle Bowey, Media Relations Manager, The Lowry**

Business background and objectives:

Set in a magnificent waterside location at the heart of the redeveloped Salford Quays in Greater Manchester, The Lowry is the National Landmark Millennium Project for the Arts and the largest millennium project outside London. The Lowry houses two theatres, bars, restaurants and several gallery spaces showing the work of LS Lowry alongside contemporary artists.

In November 1999, five months prior to opening in April 2000, The Lowry was very much a building site and still commonly perceived as just a gallery for Lowry's work. As an unknown and untested brand, The Lowry's business objectives were to communicate that it was also an important venue for the performing arts in the northwest and to persuade people to buy theatre tickets five months in advance of the theatre opening.

PR objectives:

The PR campaign needed to generate substantial regional media coverage, communicating The Lowry's significance as a venue for the northwest, the fact that the building included theatres and tickets for shows were on sale. It was also important that the box office number was communicated to generate ticket sales, enquiries and new entries for the database. The PR measurement criteria were therefore an assessment of the quality and quantity of media coverage, the numbers of enquiries generated as a result of the coverage and the number of contacts added to The Lowry database.

Strategy:

Working with a PR consultancy, The Lowry staged a media event – 'Ballerinas on a building site' – to launch the opening of the box office and the first brochure of theatre events.

To give a flavour of the variety of shows on offer at The Lowry, it was important that the event involved a diverse range of performers. Ballerinas in leotards and hard hats provided great fodder for the press photographers while a singer from Opera North performed a rendition from the *Barber of Seville* while smearing comedian Johnny Vegas in shaving foam and finally shaving his chest. The performance worked brilliantly for photographers and television crews. Manchester-born Radio 1 DJ, Mark Radcliffe, acted as unofficial spokesperson providing entertaining radio and TV interviews about the progress of the building and broadening the appeal to a younger audience.

Results and evaluation :

Media interest was phenomenal. Every local TV and radio news crew broadcast footage and interviews for the rest of the day and throughout the following day, resulting in seven local TV pieces and one national television item on BBC breakfast news. A photographer from the Press Association led to national press coverage. The Lowry also had its own photographer so that pictures could be syndicated across the region. Hundreds of press cuttings poured in over the next few weeks and went as far afield as Birmingham, due to the presence of dancers from the Birmingham Royal Ballet.

The media coverage contained the required PR messages, reinforced by mentions of the Paris Opera Ballet performing in Britain for the first time in fifteen years. This generated further interest from national media.

Over the three days following the event, the Box Office was inundated with over 1,000 phone calls. There were 100 immediate bookings for shows, generating £8,000 in revenue. This trend continued the following week resulting in Box Office takings of £10,000. Numbers on the mailing list also significantly increased with around 1,000 people registering for more information every week. The success of the event was also reflected in the numbers of general public who requested site tours of the building.

www.thelowry.com

Campaign File 6: Internal communications

BUPA – One Life

'Promoting the brand proposition outside the company could only happen when we got it right inside the company first.' – **Barry Dyer, Group Director Organisational Development, BUPA**

Business background and objectives:

BUPA had two key business objectives: to develop a more customer-orientated organisation and to improve profitability. In 1998 they launched the 'One Life' internal communications programme, designed to help achieve these goals by enabling every employee to develop their contribution to delivering BUPA's brand promise and to identify ways of improving their job satisfaction in the process.

The title 'One Life' came from the principle of the power of one, where every individual can make a difference by what they do. The programme was built on the Service Profit Chain principles developed by Earl Sasser at Harvard College. He suggested that customers and front line employees should be the top priority of service companies.

In 1999, the programme was followed by 'Leading One Life', a personal development programme aimed at BUPA's senior managers.

PR objectives:

The key PR objective was to effectively communicate the One Life and Leading One Life programmes to encourage many employees to participate. This would help ensure the success of both campaigns in terms of employee and customer satisfaction and therefore, improve financial results. These indicators would be measured by an internal audit of employee opinions, a survey of BUPA clients and financial data.

Strategy:

Prior to the launch of the One Life programme, several different tactics engaged employees with the idea that BUPA needed to change. Customer research was commissioned and shared, projects were established to look at changes to systems that frustrated customers and which prevented employees from providing excellent service. A video was produced which acted out the themes of typical complaint letters so that employees could understand the frustration that was felt by customers. This proved very effective in establishing the case for change.

One Life recognised the influence managers would have in the success of the programme. The different management teams across the whole organisation were therefore briefed on the programme's objectives and how it would work. Each manager was provided with a briefing pack containing a guidebook, booklet, summary cards and video that they could use with their own teams to discuss the programme's rationale and how it would affect them.

Prior to its launch, various methods were used to engage and stimulate intrigue about One Life, including regular feature articles in the fortnightly company magazine. Opportunities were offered for the One Life launch video so that staff who had an unusual hobby or talent could audition to take part. Finally, as the start of the programme approached, a poster campaign posed topical questions that would be explored throughout the One Life campaign.

Two venues covered the north and south of England and ran programmes simultaneously so that all twelve thousand employees could attend within three months. This was important to ensure the messages hit every employee within the shortest period possible. Towards the end key service partners and some customers were invited to attend so that they could see first hand the momentum BUPA was creating amongst its employees.

A video was produced eighteen months after the launch of the programme that described the experience of three BUPA customers based on the difference that had been made to their lives by members of staff.

'Leading One Life' was a further step in the process, designed for managers to help them reinforce the One Life values. Activities included partnering with a colleague from another part of the organisation to explore the impact their leadership style had on their team's ability to deliver excellent service.

Results and evaluation:

The three key result areas of employee satisfaction, customer satisfaction and financial performance all indicated that the employee programmes had a positive effect.

Anecdotal feedback from the participants was very encouraging and appeared to have a positive impact on their motivation, commitment and confidence. Similarly, the impact on BUPA's employee climate registered strongly. Perceptions regarding the competence and commitment of the leadership of the company improved significantly (up ten per cent from 1997–2000) as did employees' conviction regarding the organisation's customer focus (up thirteen per cent over the same period). Most impressive of all was the extent to which employees now felt the organisational culture was conducive to developing delivery of the BUPA service (up seventeen per cent).

Meanwhile, a customer survey conducted in September 2000, indicated that the number of BUPA members rating employees as 'excellent' had increased by eleven per cent since 1998. During the same period, the number of BUPA members rating overall service 'excellent' increased by twelve per cent, while eight per cent more respondents now felt 'totally confident' in BUPA.

Financial results followed a similar pattern. A modest improvement in 1999 on the previous year's performance was followed by record turnover and profits in 2000 – more than double those of 1999.

One Life has remained a strong internal brand with new initiatives building on the success and taking the values forward.

www.bupa.com

Campaign File 7: Lobbying

Vodafone plc – New HQ

'PR was an absolutely essential element in obtaining planning permission for our new world headquarters.' – **Mike Caldwell, Group Corporate Communications Director, Vodafone**

Business background and objectives:

In 1983 Vodafone had 50 employees working from one small building at its base in Newbury. By 1997 the company had grown to 3,000 employees in 51 buildings, scattered across a 4-mile radius.

The organisation decided to consolidate into one world headquarters site, which gave them an instant problem. There was only one option for development in the Newbury area – a greenfield site lying outside the town planning boundary and therefore likely to attract strong protests from environmentalists.

PR objectives:

PR was crucial to the success of the planning application, the key objective being to win public opinion and gain the support of local politicians. The targets for the campaign were local authority councillors, the local MP, local media and Vodafone employees. In addition to ultimate approval of plans, the campaign would be evaluated in accordance with attendance at events and the proportion of positive reporting in local media.

Strategy:

The PR campaign began with different messages for external and internal audiences. A tough line was taken with the media, saying that if Vodafone failed to get planning permission its continued location in Newbury could be in question. Meanwhile employees were assured that the company's first choice would be to minimise disruption and stay in the area.

Key stages in the PR campaign were marked by the planning process such as the appointment of architects, outline plans, detailed plans, models and filing for planning permission. In all, the campaign was run on a week by week basis over fifteen months.

As negative press coverage increased after the initial announcement, especially in the letters pages of the local papers, personal replies were issued to every correspondent, and every interview request was accepted to reinforce how seriously the project was taken by Vodafone.

Vodafone consulted local people and organisations widely including meetings with local politicians, business groups and members of the public. A brochure directly appealing for support was produced and distributed with all three local papers. Polling cards were also distributed asking 'Do you want Vodafone to stay in Newbury?' and 'Do you think councillors should approve the plans set out in the brochure?' Results were collated and distribution timed to gain maximum impact in the local media.

A six-week advertising campaign highlighting Vodafone's significance as a global company sparked huge debate and was followed by a major exhibition at Newbury Show with detailed models of the development and artists' impressions. Ahead of the show, a video was produced and given to staff and local councillors.

As planning permission was lodged – one year after the launch of the campaign – the poll results were issued showing overwhelming support for the project. The 7,000 supporters who had responded to the earlier poll were mailed a pre-addressed envelope in which to submit their views to West Berkshire Council.

Sixteen months into the campaign, Vodafone was dealt a major blow as planning officers recommended a refusal of the plans. This was followed by the Environment Committee voting against the project on the Chairman's casting vote.

In a final swing of public opinion, fifteen hundred staff marched through the streets and supporters were encouraged to vote in a local newspaper telephone survey – resulting in nine out of ten support. The following week, major adjustments were made to the transport plan, resulting in two out of four objections being met. A full resolution to grant planning permission on terms acceptable to Vodafone was put to the vote with a 25–18 majority in favour of the project.

Results and evaluation:

Over 4,000 people attended the Newbury Show to see the unveiling of the model and artists' impressions, including 45 out of 54 councillors. Seven thousand local people responded to the direct mail poll with 95.8 per cent voting for Vodafone to stay in Newbury and 86.6% per cent supporting the new development. The results of the pre-addressed envelope campaign helped win key support from three town councils – Newbury, Hungerford and Thatcham. Meanwhile West Berkshire Council issued its own poll findings showing that nine out of ten supported Vodafone.

Through persistent grass-roots networking and sustaining

momentum with a variety of communications methods, the campaign enlisted many supporters, resulting in local approval for the project, allowing the mobile communications giant to remain in the town where it was founded. The new world headquarters is being built at a cost of over £120 million. It will have its first occupation in 2002.

www.Vodafone.com

Featured Businesses |

Amnesty International
Baby Organix
Bupa
Carphone Warehouse
Coca Cola Great Britain
Cole & Mason
Corporate Advisory Services
Diageo
Durdle Davies
Italian Secrets
Johnson & Johnson
Matthew Clark
McVitie's
MediaAble
Metrica
Motorola
Piaggio
Prologic
Pulse Group
SDL International
Sega
Shell UK
Sourceree
TCS
The Lowry
Virgin Group
Vodafone

Featured PR Specialists |

Annie Garthwaite Communications
Edelman Worldwide
GCI London
Grayling PR
Henry's House
Julia Wherrell
Lexis PR
Midnight Communications
Red Rooster Consumer & Beauty
Strategy PR
Suzanne Howe

Useful Resources and Websites

Forward Planning

Advance Media Information	www.amiplan.com
(forward events diary/news)	
Crimson	www.crimsonuk.com
(advance TV production news and info)	
Foresight	www.fifi.co.uk/
	www.profilegroup.co.uk
Future Events News Service	http://fens.hubcom.net/fensnews/
Future News	www.futurenews.co.uk/

General Media Sites

The European Journalism Page (European media)
www.demon.co.uk/eurojournalism/media.html
Flying Inkpot International News Links   http://inkpot.com/news/
Hold the Front Page   www.holdthefrontpage.co.uk
(UK Regional Press)
Metagrid (newspaper and magazine database)   www.metagrid.com/
NewsDirectory.com   www.newsdirectory.com/
(media listings)
Newslink (US Media Listings)   www.newslink.org/
Newsrack (links to almost every online   www.newsrack.com
newspaper and magazine site around the
world)

OnlineNewspapers.com (online   www.onlinenewspapers.com/
    newspapers from around the world)
The Paper Boy   www.thepaperboy.com
    (international media database)
PubList.com   www.publist.com/
    (search facility for magazines and journals)

Online News

Associated Press Television News	www.aptn.com/
BBC News Online	http://news.bbc.co.uk/
CNN.com	www.cnn.com/
ITN	www.itn.co.uk/
The Onion (US news site)	www.theonion.com
Press Association (news gathering agency)	www.pa.press.net/
Reuters (news gathering agency)	www.reuters.com
USA Today	www.usatoday.com/

UK National Newspaper Sites

Daily Telegraph	www.telegraph.co.uk
Evening Standard	www.thisislondon.co.uk
Express	www.expressnewspapers.co.uk
Financial Times	www.ft.com
Guardian	www.guardian.co.uk
Independent	www.independent.co.uk
Mirror	www.mirror.co.uk
Observer	www.observer.co.uk
Scotsman	www.scotsman.com
Star	www.megastar.co.uk
Sun	www.currantbun.com
Sunday Times	www.the-times.co.uk
Sunday Telegraph	www.telegraph.co.uk
The Times	www.the-times.co.uk

Selected US Newspapers

New York Times	www.nytimes.com
Time	www.time.com
Wall Street Journal	www.wsj.com

Public Relations Industry

The Public Relations Society of America   www.prsa.org/
Council of Public Relations Firms USA/ICCO   www.prfirms.org/
Institute of Public Relations UK   www.ipr.org.uk/
International Association of Business
    Communicators   www.iabc.com/homepage.htm
International Public Relations Association   www.ipranet.org/
PR Week (with UK, US, Asia, Germany   www.prweek.net
    and Worldwide editions)
Public Relations Consultants
    Association UK   www.martex.co.uk/prca/
The Public Relations Institute of Ireland   www.prii.ie/
Public Relations Online   www.public-relations-online.net/

PR Resources

Advance Features   www.advancefeatures.com/
BMC Clipserver   www.clipserver.com/
Durrants media monitoring   www.durrants.net/
Editors Media Directories   www.editorsmediadirectories.com/
Hollis PR   www.hollis-pr.com/
PIMS   www.pims.co.uk/
Programme News   www.programmenews.co.uk/
Romeike Media Intelligence   www.romeike.com/
Royal Mail   www.royalmail.com/
Waymaker   www.waymaker.net/

Media Evaluation

Association of Media Evaluation Companies   www.amec.org.uk
Carma   www.carma.com
Echo   www.echoResearch.com
Metrica (media analysis and   www.metrica.net
    evaluation specialists)

Market Research

Association of Qualitative Research   www.aqr.org.uk
British Market Research Association   www.bmra.org.uk
Durdle Davies (business research specialists)   www.durdledavies.com

The Gallup Organization   info@gallup.co.uk
Market Research Society   www.mrs.org.uk

Competitions, Direct Mail and Promotions

Guidance on competition and promotional
    rules from Institute of Sales Promotion   www.isp.org.uk
Guidance on UK data protection law   www.dataprotection.gov.uk
Mail preference website   www.mpsonline.org.uk

Bibliography

Bennett, A, *How to Live on 24 Hours A Day*, George H Doran & Co., 1910

Bland, Theaker and Wragg, *Effective Media Relations*, Kogan Page, 2000

Booth, E, *Public Relations – The Best Ad Of All: Word Of Mouth*, Brand Republic (website), 2000

Covey, S R, *The 7 Habits of Highly Effective People*, Fireside (Simon and Schuster), 1989

Craven, R, *Kick-Start Your Business*, Virgin Publishing, 2001

Cumming, T, *Little e, Big Commerce*, Virgin Publishing, 2001

Fairchild M, *The Public Relations Research and Evaluation Toolkit*, IPR/PRCA, 1999

Gregory A, *Public Relations In Practice*, Kogan Page, 1996

Haig, M, *The Essential Guide to Public Relations on the Internet*, 2001

Additional Information Sources

'What Makes News?', based on original text by David Gledhill, Editor, *Bath Chronicle*

Marketing Week, Centaur Communications Ltd

Marketing, Haymarket Business Publications Ltd

PR Week, Haymarket Professional Business Publications Ltd, www.prweek.com

Richard Levick, Levick Communications (*Business Age*, October 1999)

Reputations.com, Haymarket Conferences

Steve Ellis, MediaAble Ltd, *steve@mediaable.freeserve.co.uk*

Thanks to the originator of the PR vs Advertising 'I'm good' and 'I hear you're good' graphic.

Author's note

Company names and details have been changed in three of the case studies referred to in this book (3rd Rock Organics, Picture This and Wheel Time) to protect confidentiality. However, the scenarios given are based upon real-life situations.

Index

CENTRE FOR SMALL & MEDIUM SIZED ENTERPRISES

Warwick is one of a handful of European business schools that have won a truly global reputation. Its high standards of both teaching and research are regularly confirmed by independent ratings and assessments.

The Centre for Small & Medium Sized Enterprises (CSME) is one of the school's major research centres. We have been working with people starting a business, or already running one, since 1985. The Centre also helps established companies to reignite the entrepreneurial flame that is essential for any modern business.

We don't tell entrepreneurs what to do – just help them be more aware and better informed of the opportunities and pitfalls of running a growing small enterprise.

Much of our practical knowledge is gleaned from the experience of individuals who themselves have been there and done it. These kinds of business coaches rarely commit their observations to paper, but in this Virgin/Warwick series they have captured in print their passion and their knowledge. It's a new kind of business publishing that addresses the constantly evolving challenge of business today.

For more information about Warwick Business School (courses, owner networks and other support to entrepreneurs, managers and new enterprises), please contact:

Centre for Small & Medium Sized Enterprises
Warwick Business School
University of Warwick
Coventry CV4 7AL
UK
Tel: +44 (0) 2476 523741 (CSME); or 524306 (WBS)
Fax: +44 (0) 2476 523747 (CSME); or 523719 (WBS)
Email: enquiries@wbs.warwick.ac.uk
And visit the Virgin/CSME pages via:
www.wbs.warwick.ac.uk

Also available in the Virgin Business Guides series:

LITTLE e, BIG COMMERCE
HOW TO MAKE A PROFIT ONLINE

Timothy Cumming

Now that the first wave of dotcom mania has passed, the right way to run
a website is becoming clearer. If you haven't taken the e-Commerce plunge
yet, or if you want to get more out of your website, we'll introduce you to
the world of e-customers, e-competitors and e-suppliers, taking you
through the practical steps of getting and staying online. You'll find out
what e-Commerce really is and how to do it properly – and, above all,
profitably – so you can make money instead of draining your resources.
With the expert advice in this book, you can stay ahead of this fast-moving
game.

ISBN 0 7535 0542 8

KICK-START YOUR BUSINESS
100 DAYS TO A LEANER, FITTER ORGANISATION

Robert Craven

Feel your business could do with a tune-up, but are too busy running it to sort out the problems? With the fast, proven techniques in this book, you can transform your workplace into a powerhouse. The case studies, worksheets and practical exercises will help you to take the pain out of business planning, increase your profitability and keep your customers. You'll find out how to identify your company's strengths and weaknesses and assess its potential, and learn the secret obsessions of all successful entrepreneurs.

ISBN 0 7535 0532 0

THE BEST-LAID BUSINESS PLANS
HOW TO WRITE THEM, HOW TO PITCH THEM

Paul Barrow

Planning is not just for start-ups – it's the key to successful business development and growth for every company, new or old. But once a business is up and running, it's all too easy to concentrate only on day-to-day operations. If you're launching new products and services, taking on more people, relocating to bigger premises, buying a business or selling one, you'll do it better if you plan it. This book shows you how to present the right plan for the right audience – so you stand a better chance of getting what you need. The sound practical advice, case studies and exercises in this book will help you through the planning process and ensure that yours are indeed the best-laid plans.

ISBN 0 7535 0537 1

DO SOMETHING DIFFERENT
PROVEN MARKETING TECHNIQUES TO TRANSFORM YOUR BUSINESS

Jurgen Wolff

If you carry on doing what you've been doing, you're going to carry on getting to where you've been getting. So if you want more business, you'd better *Do Something Different!* This book, built around 100 instructive and revealing case studies, contains plenty of advice on how to take charge of your situation and create your own alternatives. It's full of examples of entrepreneurs who took a sideways look at the market and their competitors, and decided to branch out and do something a little bit surprising. As a result they made their products and their companies stand out among the competition – vital in today's business environment. Engagingly written by a great individualist, *Do Something Different* will show you how to break the mould and find your way to greater success. Follow its advice and you can set yourself apart from the crowd.

ISBN 0 7535 0528 2

IT'S NOT ABOUT SIZE
BIGGER BRANDS FOR SMALLER BUSINESSES

Paul Dickinson

Branding is one of the most important aspects of marketing for any enterprise. In this straightforward guide, Paul Dickinson, who has worked to define some of the biggest brands in the world, shows how an eye for detail and design can help to re-energise any company or organisation. In this book, you'll find out how simple brand identifiers like colour and 'feel' can make powerful statements about your company, no matter what its size. Paul Dickinson shows how to change the way you think about your company's identity, and how to take simple steps to increase your sales and profits through effective branding and enhanced customer satisfaction. Fascinating case studies demonstrate how the theory has been turned into practical steps – and checklists and action plans will enable you to do the same.

ISBN 0 7535 0593 2

THE BOTTOM LINE
BUSINESS FINANCE: YOUR QUESTIONS ANSWERED

Paul Barrow

'My business is growing and profitable but how come it is always so short of cash?', 'Is it true that I could need nearly half my annual turnover just to fund my debtors and stock – and why?' The answers to these and other frequently asked questions are provided in short, easy to read and understandable sections. These are also followed by case studies, giving short insights into what other businesses have done and why it worked for them. Covering topics such as: understanding financial statements; financial analysis and control; break even analysis; profit improvement; securing the right type of funding; and buying and selling a business; *The Bottom Line* is invaluable for those running or managing a business.

ISBN 0 7535 0569 X

DOING THE BUSINESS
BOOST YOUR COMPANY'S FORTUNES

David Hall

How can you boost profits, service and efficiency in your business by using lessons from other entrepreneurs? *Doing the Business* is a workbook that entrepreneurs can dip into and use with their teams – giving them the confidence to grow, revitalise, reinvent and lead their businesses. Practical toolkits, tips and checklists, on problems such as system slippage, help you along the way and provide a systematic process supported by case examples for each issue, which inspire people to use the toolkits themselves. David Hall has taken his programme around the globe, and this book is based on the tacit wisdom of entrepreneurs the world over, particularly the UK, Australia and the USA. A book for businesspeople by businesspeople, *Doing the Business* supports entrepreneurs in a very practical, *proven* manner.

ISBN 0 7535 0680 7

20/20 HINDSIGHT
FROM STARTING UP TO SUCCESSFUL ENTREPRENEUR, BY THOSE WHO'VE BEEN THERE

Rachelle Thackray

Do you often wonder how the most innovative entrepreneurs made it to where they are today? Would you like to know how they did what they did – and what it cost? In *20/20 Hindsight*, Rachelle Thackray follows the stories of some of these entrepreneurs as they tell, in their own words, what drove them to set up the businesses they did, and what helped them trust in their own ideas. Drawing on hundreds of interviews covering a number of sectors – retail, finance, technology, design, consultancy – she includes accounts of: the initial brainwave; growth and expansion; setting up offices; forming partnerships; overcoming difficulties along the way; and what comes next? Every entrepreneur wishes they knew then what they know now. With plenty of first-person advice and checklists to chart your progress through the issues raised at each stage, with *20/20 Hindsight* you can start one jump ahead.

ISBN 0 7535 0547 9

Forthcoming Virgin Business Guides:

CUSTOMER IS KING
HOW TO EXCEED THEIR EXPECTATIONS

Robert Craven

CASHING IN
CREATE, IMPROVE AND REALISE THE VALUE IN YOUR
BUSINESS

Paul Barrow